KEMO SABE
WISDOM

PRACTICAL WAYS TO HELP YOUR BUSINESS SUCCEED

TOM YODER

ISBN: 1-448-67469-7
ISBN-13: 978-1-448-67469-5

CONTENTS:

To Nancy.

I give my most sincere thanks to my daughter Sara, who pushed me and spurred me along as only a daughter can do. She spent more time editing this book than I did writing it. This has been a fabulous father/daughter adventure.

I also want to thank two of my friends who took most of the photographs used in this book. Jeff Vanuga, from Dubois, Wyoming, is renowned as one of the premier wildlife photographers in the world. Max Helmers is one of my best friends and a terrific Cowboy who always has his camera at the ready on every ride that he takes.

Introduction

I would like you to read this book as if we were having a conversation. If we were having a cup of coffee together, I would tell you that in order to be successful in a small business the most important thing, by far, is to be absolutely certain that the customer is your priority.

I would also tell you that persistence, determination, character, and integrity are the most important assets in order to achieve success. That's why, during the course of our conversation, I would make a lot of references and comparisons to the Cowboy.

And, of course, I would throw in a few stories about our Kemo Sabe stores in Aspen and Vail, Colorado.

By keeping it simple, taking care of every customer, and doing things the Cowboy way, we have managed to do pretty well. Heck, if the team that runs Kemo Sabe can learn to succeed, then I'll flat guarantee that you can too!

Who's Running The Show?

One Saturday morning I walked into our local lumberyard and hardware store. There were four or five clerks gathered at the checkout counter at the front of the store. Note that I have labeled them "clerks" rather than salespeople. To me, clerks are people in retail who stand there and wait to take the money, with no interest in actually helping anyone.

When I asked one of the clerks about the sizes in which they sold plywood, he was way ahead of me, saying, "And I suppose that you will want us to cut it for you, right?"

"How did you know I was going ask that? And, for sure, I'd really like that, will you do it?" I answered.

"Oh, almost everyone like you asks, but normally we won't cut it."

"So, will you cut it for me?"

"That all depends on the guys in the back. I don't know if they will or not."

"Do the guys in the back decide whether you will help me out or not?"

"Yeah, that's what it comes down to. If they're in the mood you might get 'em to do it for you, but it's not up to me."

It was just as fascinating to me that the other clerks were standing by the counter passively watching the exchange. I would guess that as soon as I left they had a great time commenting on just how ridiculous customers can be.

After I paid for my four-by-eight-feet piece of plywood, I went to the yard to pick it up. The "guys in the back" were hanging out shootin' the breeze next to their fancy saws. However, they weren't quite in the right mood to help me out with a couple of cuts. Actually, they weren't even in the mood to show me where the plywood was stacked, other than pointing to a far corner of the yard. I was able to find the stack of plywood myself, but the four-by-eight sheet is still in my garage waiting for me to find a friend who will cut it into four pieces for me.

Don't You Know How Busy I Am?

For years we went to lunch at a diner down the street from Kemo Sabe. Aspen is a small town, so obviously we know them and they know us, and we've never been bashful about leaving nice tips. We have also sent literally thousands of our customers there.

One day the waitstaff accidently kept my credit card at their cash register. I didn't realize it 'til a couple of days later when we took one of our Kemo Sabe vendors to dinner at another restaurant and I didn't have my card. I went back to the diner the next day to retrieve my card, and as soon as I walked in the manager said, "Hey, I've got your credit card." When I asked why she hadn't called me, since my name and Kemo Sabe are both on the card, she replied that if she bothered to call everyone who left their card there she wouldn't have time to manage the place.

With that, a lot of the air went out of the balloon in my enthusiasm for being a big fan of hers—and that restaurant. For a long time after that, until they got a new manager, we didn't send nearly as many people there, because Kemo Sabe prefers to recommend businesses that are downright passionate about taking care of their customers.

You're Late Today? Of All Days?!?!

Central Park South is pretty much the epicenter of the New York Marathon, especially on Saturday, the day before the race. Most of the fifty thousand runners seem to make their way to the park to soak in the atmosphere and electricity. My daughter Sara and I were running the marathon, and we were among the many runners checking on a nearby Starbucks location that Saturday to find out when they opened on Sunday morning. Thousands of runners needed to board buses between 6:00 and 6:30 a.m. for transportation to the start of the race, so that's why it was so critical to find out what time they opened. I can assure you that a lot of Starbucks customers were elated to find out that they would get their morning coffee because, in fact, Starbucks opened at 6:00 a.m.

Yet, at 6:00 in the morning it was clear that the Starbucks was not going to be open on time. To add to this letdown, the staff made it pretty obvious with their hand gestures that they weren't in any huge hurry to open and that all of the people waiting outside should just go away. We heard an awful lot of formerly loyal Starbucks customers swearing that they would never patronize Starbucks again.

Who was in charge of this embarrassment of an iconic brand name? The answer, of course, was no one. Was it expecting too much to believe that a Starbucks manager, or district manager, could have been aware enough to realize that several thousand extra people would be in the area as early as 5:30 on that Sunday morning?

Then, to add fuel to the fire, Dunkin' Donuts was at the runners' village, giving away gallons of fabulous hot coffee and thousands of stocking caps. I reckon that the Dunkin' Donuts team was doing backflips with their terrific showing that day...and I wonder if Starbucks is aware of the hit they took.

Once upon a time, I became a devoted fan of Starbucks because of the way I always felt when I entered a Starbucks shop. The rich coffee aroma and the urgency of the staff to make sure each customer got the perfect coffee drink won me over time after time. Nowadays I am hearing a lot more about how profitable their instant coffee will be and how many doors they are opening every day in China, rather than about their determination to have the best baristas delivering the best coffee and a great experience to each and every customer.

A Five-Star Experience

About twenty miles down valley from Aspen is a small sandwich joint named Scottie's. Even though it is in an out of the way location, the place is legendary! Why? Because the owner, Scott Wirkler, cares about his customers.

Scott is a brilliant businessman because he gives his customers what they want, and more! Scottie's caters to us working stiffs, so he arrives everyday by 4:00 a.m. and opens the joint before 6:00. The food isn't fancy, but it is absolutely fantastic and it is *exactly* what his customers want. I often walk out of Scottie's wondering if the food was *really that good* or if it was the way that I was treated that made it so delicious. See, Scott has a way of making every one of his customers feel like a V, V, VIP. He knows nearly every one of his customers by name, and if he doesn't recognize you, he will introduce himself. If you bring a guest with you, he will take the time to introduce himself and will immediately become your friend's friend. He usually remembers exactly what you ordered the last time you were there and will ask if you want the same thing, right down to the details of "extra brown mustard?" or "with a few jalapeños?" You can take your grandmother or your two-year-old to Scottie's and be certain that they will love the place!

If you're short on cash, Scottie's is not going to turn you away. He'll just put it on your "account." And I'm willing to bet that it's a rare occurrence when he doesn't get paid back.

Because Scott runs the place so well, it is clear that every person on his staff also has their own personal commitment to be at their very best with every customer and every order. My hunch is that his training program goes something like this: "Watch me and do what I do. And most important, treat customers the way that you would like to be treated." When I leave Scottie's I always feel like I want to go to every person who works there and shake their hand and thank them for doing such a great job!

On more than one occasion, I have been with a group of people who get around to discussing local businesses, and Scottie's will often come up as the best-run business in the Aspen Valley. The bottom line is that Scott has a way of making you feel like you are the most important customer he's ever had.

Those four stories speak volumes about businesses in the US of A and how they view their customers. One would think that caring about customers would be the most elementary and fundamental concept for every business, yet based upon the experiences that we all encounter day after day, I question whether taking care of customers really is such a priority in American business after all.

Of course it would be difficult, actually next to impossible, to find a business that says, "We don't really care about our customer—we're going to run our business based upon what's easiest for us." Yet it sure does appear that many businesses *don't* care about their customers.

For those of you who are responsible for any part of a business, you had better darn well take a look at how you run your operation. If you're not putting your customer first, I would say that you need to change your focus and purpose.

I have found that achieving success in a small business is really not all that difficult, *if* you understand the most important fundamental element, which is simply to *think* about your customer.

If you put yourself in your customer's position, and think about what you, as a customer, would want from your business, then all of the other stuff will begin to fall into place.

Over the years at Kemo Sabe, I have learned that it is absolutely essential to put the customer first. It has certainly worked for us. If you can take that one piece of wisdom and advice from me and apply it to whatever business you are in, then I will pretty much guarantee that it will work for you too.

But I want you to get more from this book than the importance of "customer service." There are so many good books out there about service that you hardly need another one. I want to show you that running a business should be *fun*—for you, for your staff, and especially for your customer. And when you need a role model for doing things right and being at your best, you can't go wrong if you do things the Cowboy way.

Whenever I get the opportunity to talk with someone who is trying to make their business better, especially someone starting a business, I always want to share the secrets of what we have learned at Kemo Sabe. That's what this book is: a conversation about building a better business.

MTCFI And The COWBOY

This is not a high-tech or sophisticated "How To" manual. Rather, it is the story of a small retail store that has achieved remarkable success. Kemo Sabe has earned its success and its reputation, not through creative marketing or discounted prices, but by taking care of our customers.

At Kemo Sabe we have two specific goals that we work towards every single day:

1. MTCFI
Make The Customer Feel Important

If you make those five words the foundation of your business, you will be successful.

2. Do business with integrity. We call this the Cowboy Code.

The Cowboy is the most famous icon in America. Wherever you go on this planet they've heard of the Cowboy.

You will notice that I capitalize Cowboy…and why not? The way I look at it, if we are expected to capitalize President and Senator and Governor, then Cowboy certainly deserves the distinction as well.

I'm going to tell you about a few real Cowboys I know and why, in many ways, they are role models and inspirations for Kemo Sabe.

"Customers Rule"

We have all seen those reports and studies that tell you that the survival rate of a start-up business is a pretty grim statistic. Lots and lots of businesses do fail, that's for sure. But I'd be willing to bet that if you were to take a survey you would learn that businesses that set out with a mission of "giving the customer what they want" actually have a high success rate.

In 1994 Jeff Bezos acted on his belief that online shopping could be a reality and founded *amazon.com.* He named his dream *"amazon"* because the Amazon River basin supports more varied forms of life than all of the other places on this planet combined. But far more than *amazon.com* being a tech-driven success story, it is based upon, and fueled by, a passion for customer service. The first two points in *amazon's* company values are:

· *Customer Obsession: We start with the customer and work backwards.*

· *Innovation: If you don't listen to your customers you will fail. But if you only listen to your customers you will also fail.*

This is the greatest formula for success that I could ever imagine.

Of course Jeff Bezos had a spectacular business plan and *amazon* is extremely high-tech, but from day one his company was, and still is, based upon one fundamental principle: "Customers Rule." Years ago Jeff came into Kemo Sabe, and when he signed the door that we sometimes invite friends of Kemo Sabe to sign, he wrote *"Customers Rule"* next to his name. Over the years Jeff and his team at *amazon* have proven that they are fanatics about taking great care of their customers.

In my opinion, the *real* reason that Jeff Bezos and *amazon* have been so phenomenally successful is not a result of the internet boom. Rather, success should be attributed to *amazon's* commitment to their customers. I am a huge fan of *amazon*, and it is not because I am fortunate enough to call Jeff my friend. It is because I am convinced that *amazon* really and truly cares about me as a customer.

Do yourself a favor and order something from *amazon.com*. You will learn firsthand what a true customer-driven business is.

If You Don't Know Where You're Going, Then Any Road Will Get You There

My wife, Nancy, and I started Kemo Sabe in Snowmass Village, Colorado, in the fall of 1990. The truth is that we weren't smart enough business people, or good enough retailers, to hit the water if we had fallen out of the boat. But we did know one thing: we were determined to succeed by making the customer the most important part of Kemo Sabe.

Kemo Sabe was actually born in Colorado Springs when a local legend and furniture store owner, Bob Telmosse, started MegaMart. This was comprised of a bunch of mom-and-pop operators who ran small booths on the weekends in a giant warehouse. MegaMart gave dreamers like us a chance to own a small (very, very small—an eight-by-ten-foot booth) business. Nancy and I were among the first to sign on with Bob's refined version of a flea market, and we called our "store" Zoomies because that was the nickname for cadets at the nearby United States Air Force Academy. And what a store we had, with disposable hand-warmers, neon shoelaces, and our anchor merchandise line: fish ties. Even though MegaMart lasted only a couple of months, we got to taste a little bit of the excitement that comes with owning a store.

Shortly after that, we fell into the opportunity to lease a small space in Snowmass Village, Colorado, and Nancy came up with the name Kemo Sabe. We loved the name because:

· It's Western.

· It's a feel-good name from the black-and-white TV days of the Lone Ranger.

· It means *"trusted scout"* and *"faithful friend."*

The first month in business Kemo Sabe did $1,281 in sales. That included several days without making a sale, and other days when we did only a few dollars. In those early days of Kemo Sabe we still sold fish ties. We also carried swimsuits because we figured that people on ski vacations would want to get in the hot tub, but that they would forget to bring their suits on a ski trip. No, you certainly couldn't call Nancy and me retail geniuses. But we did one thing right that is absolutely essential in building a small store: we put the customer first.

Actually, treating our customers well was pretty easy for us, mainly because we made it fun for a customer to shop in our store. Over time, we began to create our own style of customer service, which has now become part of our Kemo Sabe brand.

That first year Kemo Sabe had two employees: Nancy and me. We were the accounting department, the shipping and receiving department, the buying team, and of course, the sales associates. As I look back on it, we learned more about "giving the customer what they want" than I could ever put into words. There is simply no substitute for being face to face with your customer.

We weren't afraid to try all kinds of different merchandise in our 400-square-foot space. We learned how to determine whether or not new products were right for our customer within a short amount of time. And when I say short, I mean within one day. If our customer didn't like these new goods, we would try something else. But if our customer did like that product, then we would be off and running.

The first year we were in business, we were persuaded by some friends to carry a line of Swiss skin care products. We had to invest a decent amount of money and effort to secure the rights to represent the line in Snowmass, and it really was a superb product. But Kemo

Sabe was pretty much the opposite of what people expect in a skin care shopping experience, and we quickly realized from the reaction of our customers that we had made a mistake. So, even though we had made quite an investment, including our pride, we changed our course on the kind of merchandise that we should carry at Kemo Sabe.

I clearly remember another time when we bought a dozen cotton sweaters that retailed for $66. On the very first day that those sweaters arrived, we sold nine of them. We called the supplier that evening and had twenty-four more shipped so that they would arrive the next day. During that ski season we sold a few hundred of them and Nancy and I thought that those sweaters were a huge success—until we learned from a customer that they lost their shape after wearing them just once or twice. After that, when customers came in wanting to buy more of those sweaters, we took a lot of pride in letting them know that we were no longer carrying them because we didn't believe that they were high enough quality for our customer and, thus, for Kemo Sabe!

This sweater experience was also the beginning of a major change that shaped the future of Kemo Sabe. Not only did it make us question why Kemo Sabe was in the sweater business at all, it also made us question why were we carrying fish ties, swimsuits, or any other stuff that could be found at thousands of shops around the country. Since we were both enamored with the West, we decided that what we really wanted, and what we would be best at, would be to turn Kemo Sabe into a Western store. It goes without saying that it was one of the best decisions that we ever made!

That first winter was also when I realized how much I love being in the Hat business. At first, I ordered eight inexpensive fabric Hats that were kind of an Indiana Jones–type look. I discovered that a whole lot of people would love to wear a Hat, if only they were able find a look that would be right for them. I realized that I had a talent for helping people select a shape and color that matched their style and personality. But what I enjoyed most was watching them leave our store with a little more confidence and swagger because of their Hat. Over that ski season we sold several dozen of those Hats, and even though our commitment to Hats is far more sophisticated at Kemo Sabe today, it was the beginning of a fabulous adventure for me.

(I also always capitalize the word Hat. If a person is wearing a Hat, it is always the first thing you notice and remember about their attire, regardless of whatever else they have on, including an expensive coat, a fancy watch, or even beautiful boots. Hats are my favorite piece of Kemo Sabe merchandise, and we can trace a good part of our success to the passion and dedication that we have given to Hats—not the least of which has been our determination to be better than good…to be great. More on that later.

When you look at photographs from the 1940s and '50s you will see that practically every man in America was wearing a Hat, whether he was on the streets of New York City, at a football game, or boarding an airplane. Harry Truman himself would seldom be caught outside without some type of snappy Hat. But in 1961 JFK took office and refused to wear a Hat, and just like that, the Hat business went to hell in a handbasket. This is not a good thing, because wearing a dress Hat is a fabulous way for a man—and certainly a lady too—to add a lot of class to his or her appearance.

But baseball caps don't count! First of all, these are caps, not Hats. It always gets to me when I see a well-dressed businessman dressed to the nines in a tailored suit and expensive shoes, wearing a ball cap. I guess ball caps are so prevalent these days, wearing one for any occasion has almost become acceptable, but if he were wearing a nice fedora…well, his appearance and swagger would go way, way up.)

Back to the history of Kemo Sabe. Not only were we able to learn about running a business from our customers, we also found another terrific source of inspiration and motivation from one of our vendors. Our very first supplier was Bruce Erickson of Chacon Belts from Chacon, New Mexico. Bruce should have his picture in the dictionary next to "small business." Successful small business owners generally seem to have one thing in common: somewhere, deep down inside, they realize that persistence and determination will overcome what they may lack in experience, skill, and financial resources. Bruce has been with us every step of the way and is still one of our faithful friends of Kemo Sabe, in addition to being one of our most treasured suppliers.

In the early 1970s Bruce pulled out of Detroit in an old clunker with bald tires, with only one asset to bank his future on:

determination. He needed to figure out where and how he could find satisfaction and drove throughout the West searching for his dream. We he got to the top of Holman Hill and looked into the Mora Valley of New Mexico, he knew he had found his home.

When he first moved to Chacon, population 220, it wasn't easy for him because he was practically the only gringo within a fifty-mile radius. Bruce had done some leatherwork when he was growing up, so he bought some leather scraps and a few tools, rolled up his sleeves, went to work, and named his business Dynamite Leather. Bruce and his wife and kids lived in his little leather shop, which was an old cabin. A few years later he was able to move the shop into the high-rent district of Chacon, paying twenty bucks a month for an old one-room schoolhouse. Over time, Bruce won the hard-earned respect of locals for miles around. Heck, in 1990, New Mexico Governor Garrey Carruthers himself made a special trip to Chacon to thank Bruce for the wonderful inspiration that he was to the community.

Bruce changed the name from Dynamite to Chacon Leather in 1986 when he added sterling silver buckles that he designed and produced to his line of fine belts. Now, nearly forty years later, Bruce Erickson is one of the most popular and most highly respected people in Mora County. And representing Chacon Belts is a source of pride for retailers in the Western industry. Chacon certainly makes a superb product, but when I listen to other retailers talk about how proud they are to carry Chacon in their stores, the emphasis is always about the high caliber of business that Chacon is, and the integrity of Bruce Erickson.

In addition to learning from our customers and suppliers, Nancy and I were also discovering another essential lesson: the importance of setting goals. Since our very first week in business, we set goals for each day. When we started in 1990, Nancy and I figured that we could do around $300 per day in sales. So we would set our sales goal for $125 on Monday, Tuesday, and Wednesday, but beef up our goal to $450 on Friday and Saturday. Well, you don't need to be a math whiz to figure out that since we sold only $1,218 that first month, we were a long way from hitting our target. But we did know where we wanted to go, and we learned how to set realistic goals and how to actually achieve them.

Since then we've refined our goal-setting process. Now, *everyone* at Kemo Sabe, no matter what their position, is asked to start their day, week, and season with goals on how to be at their very best, not just with sales, but with customers and as a member of the Kemo Sabe team.

One of my favorite sayings is, "If you don't know where you're going, then any road will get you there." It's such a terrific philosophy that it has become our marching orders at Kemo Sabe, and I hear our managers applying this attitude every day. Rather than being driven by the dollar amount of daily sales, we have daily huddles to review how we can be a great store that day. These brief meetings usually focus on making us a better store by improving on our knowledge and expertise, which in turn will allow us to deliver better customer service. We learned a long time ago that sometimes we could actually do a lot of business on a day when we were not at our best. But those high-dollar days don't satisfy us nearly as much as giving our customers a great experience so that they will be sure to come back.

You won't find an NFL coach yelling at his players in training camp to go out there and "Win!...Win!!...Win!!!" No, he is going to have his team working on the *fundamentals* of the game, which will lead to winning. In our case the fundamentals were simple. We focused on our own brand of customer service, and success followed.

Showdown At The Chili Shoot-Out

A tipping point day for Kemo Sabe occurred in the summer of 1992 when I attended a meeting of the Snowmass Resort Association. Part of the discussion was about the Snowmass Chili Shoot-Out, which was coming up in a few weeks. Nearly every Snowmass restaurant had entered and they were lobbying to hold the Shoot-Out from 2:00 'til 5:00 p.m., rather than making it an all-day event. With this schedule, they reasoned, they would not have to sacrifice any of their normal lunch and dinner business that Saturday. That just didn't make sense to me and it didn't take me long to object, saying that it was preposterous to think that they could expect their restaurant patrons to eat lunch, eat chili at the Shoot-Out, and then come back again for dinner. I wanted them to sacrifice a meal or two with the goal of hosting a fantastic event and causing our guests to experience such a great day in Snowmass that they would come back. The discussion got pretty heated, and even though we weren't even entered at the time, I ended up betting every restaurant a hundred bucks that Kemo Sabe would beat them in the chili competition.

Neither Nancy nor I knew anything about cooking chili but we were determined to win, so we went about things a little differently: we made the Chili Shoot-Out customer the center of attention at our booth. We had poured our batch into a giant barrel and stirred it with a six-foot stick, and we enlisted our patrons and their kids' help in stirring it. We wanted their opinions about our chili, and asked them to taste everyone else's, and tell us how we ranked. We also posted our "secret" recipe for our Kemo Sabe chili for everyone to see. (You'll see it on page 16).

In fact, we did have the best pot of chili, in part because we started making our batch three days earlier on the stove of our studio apartment. As far as we could determine, the restaurants didn't make that kind of special effort and didn't start their chili 'til that Saturday morning. We won by a landslide. I never actually collected the hundred dollars from any restaurant, but Nancy and I did confirm what we already knew about running a small business: make it about the customer.

The next summer all the restaurants got together and came up with a new rule: that no one could enter the Shoot-Out unless they were a Snowmass restaurant and actually cooked their chili in a licensed Snowmass restaurant kitchen. Even though Kemo Sabe had proven that we would give the customer a great experience, the restaurants were still determined to make the event about *them*, rather than about the customer. So, our great friends Bob and Annie Hite, who owned nearby Hite's Restaurant, lent us their kitchen and we entered as bandits. We bought hundreds of Lone Ranger masks and gave them out to people who tasted our chili, warning them that they would need a disguise if they cast a write-in vote for us, the Kemo Sabe bandits, who were not allowed to even enter the Shoot-Out. We received about 90 percent of the votes, and again, won in a landslide.

By the next summer, we knew how important it was to have fun and put on a good show. That year, right up until three minutes before the Shoot-Out began, our booth was empty and we started the rumor that Kemo Sabe wasn't going to show up. Then our shills started beating metal pots and pans with wooden spoons. We had everyone in the mall clapping and whistling and yelling—I swear, it was like a concert crowd anticipating the rock star to come onto the stage. Then, here we came, bolting out of Hite's front door, falling down the stairs and spilling a twenty-gallon barrel full of our championship chili. Of course it was staged—it was fake chili and we showed up with our real batch just in time to win the Shoot-Out again. Heck, that year they didn't even bother to count the votes.

The following year, Kemo Sabe had moved from Snowmass to Aspen and we retired from the chili competition. For a change, those restaurants in Snowmass were mighty happy with us.

Actually, there was even a little more to that last year of the Shoot-Out. I hired an old Cowboy from Texas, Gary Henry, to bring his trained Texas longhorn, Bubba, to the Shoot-Out. We were smart enough not to ask the Snowmass honchos for their permission or approval, because they would have certainly said "no way." But Bubba was a sensational hit for Snowmass and for Kemo Sabe. It was fantastic marketing for Kemo Sabe because most folks have never had the opportunity to get up close and personal with a giant Texas longhorn. We let people sit on Bubba and get their picture taken with him—for *free*, of course. Nancy and I had so much fun riding him around and actually bringing him into our shop, where he took up half the space, that it inspired us to get our own longhorn for Kemo Sabe. We named him Bo and he became one of the most popular celebrities in Snowmass and Aspen. Even now, years after he retired, people are always asking me about Bo and reminding me of one crazy thing or another that they saw us do together.

Our success in the Chili Shoot-Out was an amazingly important step in the evolution of Kemo Sabe. Looking back on it, I know that we didn't realize at the time the impact that it would have on the DNA of Kemo Sabe. The understatement is that our involvement in the Chili Shoot-Out certainly was a tipping point in building the culture of Kemo Sabe. Here's why:

· It reminded Nancy and me that having fun and actually enjoying our business is an important element in building success.

· It reinforced our belief that making the customer our priority is the key to building success.

· We realized that having our customers involved in Kemo Sabe was incredibly rewarding to us. We started hearing how much people appreciated our Kemo Sabe atmosphere and Western hospitality on the very afternoon of our first Shoot-Out.

Because of their encouragement, our relationship with customers and friends of Kemo Sabe has continued for the past twenty years. We learned that building a *relationship* with our customer would be a cornerstone for everything we do at Kemo Sabe.

· And most important, we were reminded that making immediate gains is hardly the way to build lasting success. Remember how our involvement in the Chili Shoot-Out began in the first place? I was opposed to having the Shoot-Out for three hours in the afternoon under the premise that the local restaurants could still count on their normal lunch and dinner business. I knew that was a bad plan because the customer was *not* the priority. If the Snowmass restaurants would have made it a goal to provide great customer service for the entire day, each restaurant, and all of Snowmass, would have ultimately benefitted far more in the long run. The lesson of giving our customers our very best, often without an immediate gain, has stayed with us throughout the years at Kemo Sabe.

The following is Cowboy poet Bill Jones' version of the Chili Shoot-Out from his book *The Pretzel Hold*. You'll also hear more about Bill Jones later in this book.

SNOWMASS YUPPIE TALK

Last summer I attended the Snowmass, Colorado, Great Chili Shoot-Out. Basically, the deal is to see how much chili you can eat for the $10 entry fee. It is the deal of the century, especially if you like chili. There are some prizes for the folks who cook up the best pot.

My friend, Tom Yoder, has won the first prize two years in a row. He cooks his chili in a 55-gallon oil drum and stirs it with a hoe handle. Yode makes chili kind of like porcupines make love—slowly and very carefully. Yode's chili is tongue-slappin' good but a tad on the spicy side.

"Is this chili hot?" I asked Yode.

"Nah," Yode said, "it ain't hot."

I took a spoonful and learned quick what one of them philosophers might call one of your basic truths, which is: never believe nobody in a cowboy hat that says the chili ain't hot.

Folks, that chili was the nearest thing to liquid fire I ever put in my mouth. It raised a blister on my lip and I couldn't breathe. Got the hiccups and couldn't talk. Yode looked on, happy as a dead pig in a mud hole.

"Good, ain't it?" he says.

Lucky for me Yode is a decent fellow and keeps a washtub full of beer and ice next to the chili pot. He don't charge for the beer, though I'm sure he could get $25 a bottle easy.

I guess I should have been suspicious after seeing that pile of two-foot-long hoe handles next to the chili pot. Yode says they just don't make hoe handles like they used to.

Later, a group of hands from a local ranch came by and ate about half a dozen bowls apiece. They suffered no ill effects, but the next morning the Snowmass Volunteer Fire Department got called out to their ranch. It seems the boys accidentally set the bunkhouse outhouse on fire. I didn't ask for details and I ain't real sure I want to know.

Anyways, after a great deal of begging, I got the recipe for the chili from Yode and want to "share" (Snowmass yuppie talk) it with you.

Kemo Sabe Chili

Meat from a dead cow
Meat from a dead hog
Dried red ants
Cigar ashes
Squished tomatoes
Onions
Chili rojo
South of the Border stuff
Armadillo parts
Assorted roadkill
Beer
Unknown ingredients (actually known…but secret)
Stir With A Hoe Handle

Into A Bigger Pasture: Aspen

As you can sense, we were becoming a popular little store in Snowmass and were beginning to actually build a brand. But we would sometimes hear comments in our store that would really bother us. People would be looking around and we would hear someone in the group whisper, "Don't buy anything here. Wait 'til we get to Aspen." At the time, there were actually six stores in Aspen that featured Western merchandise. Nancy and I believed that Kemo Sabe was better than any of those Aspen stores, but the fact is that Aspen, not Snowmass, is truly a shopping mecca. We knew that at some point, we would need to move Kemo Sabe to Aspen. We looked at all kinds of retail spaces in Aspen but we always found something that caused us to pass on every potential space and keep looking. Then, around noon on a Tuesday in February of 1993, we got a call saying that Bert Bidwell, the owner of a building on the best corner in Aspen, was having second thoughts about leasing a space to a large California-based retailer. Bert had been in Aspen for many years and believed that if he could find a local mom-and-pop operation then it would be nice to give them a chance. That was the break that we needed.

Bert was known, hands down and with no competition, as the gruffest, meanest man in Aspen, so we were careful to be on our best behavior in his office. We must have gotten along with him pretty well because the "interview" ended with Bert pointing a finger at us and saying, "Okay, I'll rent you the space, but I'm scheduled to sign with the California people at noon tomorrow, so you have to get everything signed and back to me by 11:00, including a check for two months' rent. Got it?"

Well, we didn't *have* the money. Nor did we have an attorney who could review the lease, or a commitment from a bank that would support us opening a store in Aspen. But we did know that this was our chance. So, we took a risk and extended ourselves way beyond what our cash flow could realistically support, and the next morning Nancy and I signed on with Bert. Was this the responsible way to grow our business? Of course not, and I am not recommending it. But we realized that this was our opportunity, and we were so determined that we knew that somehow we would make it work.

Over the years, we got to know Bert quite well, and the three of us became friends, with a lot of respect for one another. Even though we sometimes disagreed on small issues, Bert loved Aspen and was committed to having nothing less than top-shelf tenants in his building. I have never met a more honest man in my life. It's hard to give a person a higher compliment than that.

As the word spread that Kemo Sabe was moving to Aspen we got plenty of advice from our "friends." Almost all of them, except Bob and Annie Hite, said pretty much the same thing: "You are making a big mistake. Those Western stores in Aspen are going to bury you and you are not going to be able to pay the rent." Actually, those were words of encouragement to us. Nancy would always say the same thing: "Failure is not an option." She still says those same words today.

Now when we look at the first photos of our Aspen store it was like we had taken a step backwards. In Snowmass we had only 400 square feet, but we had earned a great reputation with a ton of loyal customers, and the store had taken on its own character and personality. In Aspen we had three times the space—maybe too much space for our limited finances—and not enough money to make any major leasehold improvements. Remember, there were *six* other Western stores in town, and most of them had stuff like leather-covered walls and fireplaces, which meant that they had plenty of money and resources. Plus, Aspen was going through a transformation away from mom-and-pop shops to exotic, world-renowned stores with gold leaf notations on their windows boasting of their stores in New York, Paris, Milan, and Rodeo Drive. Next to those stores, Kemo Sabe looked like a hot dog stand parked next to Tiffany. Yet Nancy and I were actually extremely fortunate because we had one fabulous advantage: we were working so darn hard that we didn't have time to look around and see what an uphill climb we were facing.

After a year in Aspen we got a big break when our friends from Snowmass, Bob and Annie Hite, sold their restaurant and Bob agreed to come work at Kemo Sabe. What we were best at, and honestly I'd challenge any small business to be much better than we were, was customer service. We were fanatics at making our customers feel special. Bob and Nancy and I developed this incredible teamwork with absolute trust in each other. We pretty much knew what the other one was up to before he or she realized it himself. We had some acts that always began spontaneously, but grew into great routines...for us and our customers. My favorite was when we had a packed store, and we were trying to help a lady who just couldn't make up her mind about buying a Stetson. We would turn off all of the lights and music in the store, so that people probably thought that we were having a power outage or closing for the evening. Then we would shine a spotlight on the lady and ask all of the other customers whether she looked:

A) Bad

B) Okay

C) Good

D) Absolutely terrific in the Hat.

Well, of course "D" always won unanimously with all kinds of whoopin' and hollerin'. Then we would crank up that classic old song "I Want to be a Cowboy's Sweetheart," and we'd have a store full of people having a terrific time...with the most ecstatic of all being the lady who just bought a new Hat—or had it purchased *for* her by some guy in the store.

What Is "CUSTOMER SERVICE" Anyway?

At Kemo Sabe we break down customer service into two parts:

1. **Knowledge**
2. **Make The Customer Feel Important**

Most of the goods we carry require a great deal of knowledge and expertise. We are not going to have much success selling a $700 Hat, a $2,000 pair of boots, or a $4,500 sterling silver buckle if all we can say is, "It's very nice" or "You'll like it." No, we need to know everything about every piece of merchandise in our store. That's why we are fanatics at having a knowledgeable and professional staff. Our training involves many segments, including written material, detailed coaching, role-playing, and on-the-job reviews. And our training never ends. We are constantly badgering and inspiring each other, trying to figure out how we could have been a little better with a customer. We *all* do it to each other—our store manager, Wendy Kunkle, challenges Nancy or me, and experienced sales associates dare new associates to improve. Anyone with a legitimate observation is encouraged to speak up. If you have a thin skin you're going to have a difficult time being on our Kemo Sabe team.

And we expect everyone at Kemo Sabe to challenge themselves to keep learning, and to push themselves to keep getting better and better. When someone is going through Kemo Sabe training I will always ask them, "Who is your boss?" Of course they will stumble on this question and there will be an awkward moment before they answer, "You are" or "Wendy is." Occasionally, someone who is thinking outside the box will say, "Well, the customer is!"

But then I will explain to them that if they are really going to succeed at Kemo Sabe they need to understand that they are really *their own* boss. The point that I try to make is that we can't possibly force them to do their very best and to be committed to their own success. That choice is really up to the individual. If each person on our team can look himself in the mirror at the end of the day and know that he did his best, I know Kemo Sabe and each of us will be a grand champion.

A perk for our staff is an "advanced training" field trip to the Stetson plants in Longview and Garland, Texas, the Lucchese factory in El Paso, and the Bohlin Silver facilities in Dallas. This is quite a challenge for Kemo Sabe because it involves getting twelve or fifteen of us from Colorado to several locations in Texas. Obviously it's difficult and very expensive, but we've always felt like it was worth the price. We all learn on these trips—not just about our products, but also about the legendary brands in the Western industry, and about working together as a team.

When a member of our sales staff graduates from our training program, he or she is a true expert. I don't know of any other stores that are quite as committed to having such a knowledgeable staff, and we are mighty proud of that.

I'd guess if you ask a lot of salespeople to define customer service, they might say it's about being friendly, courteous, and helpful. Of course we agree with that, but those qualities are so elementary that we breeze right past them. We believe that being able to *use knowledge to help the customer* is the true essence of customer service. Think of it this way: if you need technical help with your cell phone or computer, isn't it more important to have confidence in the knowledge of the person helping you, rather than feeling like he or she is "pleasant" and being "nice" to you?

We once had an employee in our Vail store who was absolutely the friendliest person you could ever meet. The way she smiled and greeted you with a "Howdy" would knock your socks off. Within a few minutes she would know where you were from, all about your kids, and the names of your pets. We would get notes telling us that she was the nicest person they had met in Colorado. But no matter how hard we tried, we were never successful in getting her beyond being friendly and becoming a *professional*. So, very few of the friends she made ever got to the point of becoming customers. Even though she was incredibly *friendly*, she never mastered the skill of using *knowledge* to develop relationships and create loyal customers.

We recognize that our customers deserve world-class customer service. And we are committed to delivering it.

Make The Customer Feel Important

Nancy and I are always analyzing and comparing the service we get from other businesses, using our experiences to define how we want things done at Kemo Sabe. Actually, I compare Kemo Sabe to just about *everything*. Sometimes this is enough to drive Nancy nuts, but I enjoy making these comparisons and I know that we have become a better business because of it. I'm not suggesting that a small business owner needs to be as much in love with their business as I am with mine, but it sure won't hurt if you are.

Generally, the bottom line is this: did they make me feel important? We began to use those five words in training our staff: *Make The Customer Feel Important, or MTCFI*. MTCFI has become our motto and our goal at Kemo Sabe. We have reminders posted in the stores and we never have any kind of staff meeting without bringing up MTCFI.

To us, MTCFI has everything to do with how we interact with our customers. Here are some of my favorite examples of how we've brought MTCFI to life over the years:

★ We are fanatics about showing the customer our merchandise the best way we possibly can. With boots, for example, there are several steps we take before the customer even gets to try the boots on. First, we kneel on the floor or sit on a low seat, face to face with the customer. Then we hold the new boot with both hands, inspect the leather, feel all around the outside of the boot, and then slide a hand into the boot to be sure that there aren't any kinds of packing material, sharp edges, or tarantulas in there. At the same time, we are talking about the quality of the skins, how the boot is made, and the workmanship involved. Then, we explain how the boots should fit, and that the correct fit will actually vary with the type of skin from which the boot is made.

We do this because we understand that many of our customers have never had the pleasure of wearing a fabulous, and expensive, pair of boots. We want to make them feel comfortable—even before they decide to buy them.

During this experience we always apply our "Rule of Three," which means that we bring a minimum of three pairs of boots back from the stockroom. Why? Because we want to offer choices. We do this even if the customer has decided on a style. All of our boots are handmade, so no two pairs ever have exactly the same look, feel, and fit. Why wouldn't we let the customer choose from several pairs of the "same" boot so that they can get the pair that is best for them?

★ When interacting with customers, even when we're not talking about our goods, we make sure that we are talking about the customer, and *not* about us. For example, we want our customer to tell us how his day skiing was, rather than making him have to listen to us describe our skiing. We want our customers to tell us about *their* kids and *their* dogs and *their* horses. We want to give our customer a chance to tell us more about who he is and what his life is like.

★ We make the effort to actually think like a customer. This must be on the same level of difficulty as those crocodile hunters who tell you that the secret is to "just think like a crocodile." I say that because a lot of small businesses sure don't seem to think like a customer. Why would a store cover its front door with "NO" signs? "NO food or drink allowed." "NO credit cards." "NO out-of-state checks." "NO dogs allowed." Your front door should actually *welcome* people to your business. I can't understand the small business attitude that basically says to people, "We'll do business with you, but it will be on *our* terms, not yours."

★ Remember my earlier example of customer service that involved the diner keeping my credit card? Well, at Kemo Sabe we are adamant that if we somehow end up with a customer's card, it is *our* fault, not the customer's. We train our staff to be certain that they have always safely returned the card.

But mistakes happen, and if we do accidentally keep a customer's credit card, it sets off a chain reaction that reflects Kemo Sabe at our best. Obviously, if the customer is in our database, getting in contact with him is relatively easy. But if we don't know the person, we try to figure out where he was going, or maybe we know someone who was with him in the store. Our salesperson will literally walk around town, searching other stores and restaurants for the cardholder. We may call local hotels to see if he is staying there. Or we call Visa, MasterCard, or AmEx and explain the situation, and they may be able to help us track the card member down. And it works—I don't think we've ever failed to find a person whose card we accidently kept.

★ Our Hats provide another opportunity for us to deliver knockout customer service through our expertise. But it can be tricky. A lot of people walk in and grab the first Hat they can get their hands on and plop it on their head. We're not particularly fond of this because the odds of them getting the right size or the best style for them are pretty slim. We've learned that once a customer puts on a Hat that doesn't fit, or is not the right style, it's pretty hard to get him to keep an open mind.

As a way to improve the odds that they grab the right size, we keep our small and large sizes away from the customer's reach. That way, we give ourselves a fighting chance to earn our credibility with the customer.

We dedicate an enormous amount of effort into being able to recognize how to figure out what Hat, including color and shape, will work best for a person. We are experts and we really do want to help, so this is a great way of getting started.

New customers often say stuff like, "Oh, you're just saying I look good in this Hat 'cause you want to sell it to me." That is not true and we actually take some offense when we hear it. I can assure you that we do not try to *sell* our goods. However, we are passionate about helping you *buy* our merchandise. This is especially true with Hats. We have come to accept that many people just don't want to wear a Hat. That's fine, because if you don't want to wear a Hat, then we are not going to try to "sell" you one. For example, a lot of times when someone buys a Hat they ask to take it home in the box. When that happens we will stop right there and say, "Sorry, but you can't have the box." We then explain that we are concerned that the Hat may end up in the box rather than on their head or hanging in their den or office. Trust me, it would be a lot easier if we sent the Hat boxes out with customers, rather than us having to recycle them, but we are such fanatics about having people use and enjoy their Hats that we can't, in good conscience, let them take the box. When you are not using your new TV, do you keep it in the box? And if you did, how often would you go to the trouble of taking it out of the box to watch it? Even if our customers don't actually wear their Hats all that often, we want them to have them hanging in their den or next to the door to remind them of Kemo Sabe and the West.

★ We often have people come in who have bought a Hat at another store, but it just isn't the right Hat for them. Trust me, wearing the "wrong" Hat is a very common occurrence. When someone has on the "wrong" Hat, here's what we do: First, we try to take the edge off by telling him how swell it is that he is wearing a Hat. Then, we'll ask if he would object to us working a little Kemo Sabe magic on it. Convincing him that we want to *help* him requires some finesse, skill, and experience, and it occasionally produces some awkward results. Still, we are willing to live dangerously for the sake of the great American West.

We are also eager to help you with your boots. We're very good at spiffing them up by rubbing leather conditioner into the leather or putting a good shine on them. We also have the experience and tools to allow your boots to fit you better, so that you can truly enjoy them.

The same goes with silver buckle sets. With our sophisticated equipment and experience, we can make a well-worn buckle set look brand new.

Sometimes people will ask what we charge to work on their Hat, boots, belt, or buckle, and the answer, of course, is nothing. We fix up close to a dozen items nearly every day, most of which weren't purchased in our store, and we are really proud of that. Not only do we get a "feel-good kick" out of it, we also know it's a great step in developing a relationship with our customer.

★ People are always asking us about celebrities who visit Kemo Sabe. Sure, we do get more than our fair share of celebrities because we are in Aspen and because Kemo Sabe is sort of a "must see" destination. But we sure don't go jumping through flaming hoops when big shots come in. In fact, it's pretty much the opposite, because we give people with notoriety a lot of space. We do have a lot of celebrities who shop at Kemo Sabe, but we don't talk about them. The result seems to be that celebs tend to feel comfortable when they are in our store.

We have had some downright funny things happen when celebrities are around, like visitors asking where the best place to catch a glimpse of so-and-so would be, yet that very person is standing right there, looking quite different in "the real world." It's not all that unusual for a very well-known celebrity to be in the store for a long time and never get bothered by anyone! I know how corny this may sound, but we want every one of our customers to feel like a celebrity in our store.

Yoder and Nancy
Photo: Brian Porter

Nancy on Bo, 1995

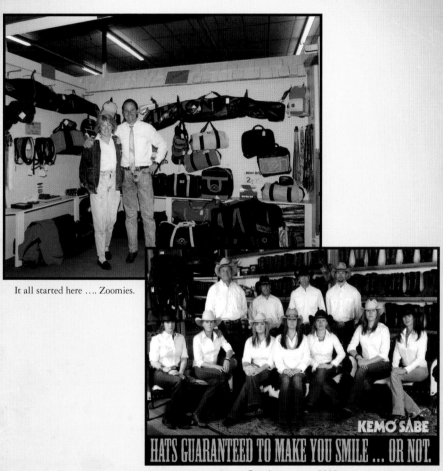

It all started here …. Zoomies.

HATS GUARANTEED TO MAKE YOU SMILE … OR NOT.

KEMO SABE

Our Aspen team, 2008
Photo: Brian Porter

We've made a gazillion friends here… Kemo Sabe Aspen today
Photo: Brian Porter

Kemo Sabe Vail, looking
up Bridge Street
Photo: Vail Chamber and
Business Association

Kemo Sabe logo on leather

Gina, Nancy,
Yoder, and Sara

Wendy with Oakley, her Buckskin Mustang

Nancy is the heart and soul of Kemo Sabe and
never loses sight of our purpose. She is loaded with
determination and fortitude, and since day one has been the
compass for our Kemo Sabe adventure
Photo: Max Helmers

Gina
Photo: Jeff Vanuga

Gina and Yoder in the high country of Wyoming
Photo: Jeff Vanuga

Yoder and his favorite pardner, Frank,
in the East Fork of the Yellowstone
River in Wyoming
Photo: Max Helmers

Cowboy coffee break
Photo: Jeff Vanuga

Yoder and Rowdy in
the Fourth of July
Parade in Aspen

Make The Customer Feel Important!

Becoming A Brand In Aspen

After a few years in Aspen, Kemo Sabe was becoming a well-known store. The biggest reward for Nancy and me was the personal satisfaction of knowing that we were running a good business. We had developed a loyal team and excellent relationships with our suppliers. Kemo Sabe was building a reputation, one day at a time and one customer at a time. Before we knew it, there were no longer six other Western stores to compete with. The ones that dropped off blamed the fact that Western was no longer "en vogue" and that the Cowboy was "out of style." Funny thing, Nancy and I have never thought of Kemo Sabe, or the Cowboy, as a fashion or trend. We have always believed that most Americans have an inner passion for the West, and we do our best to connect Kemo Sabe with the American West and the Cowboy. Actually, because we believe so strongly in this, it's one of the easiest things that we do.

There is an old axiom that says, "Nothing's good for business like good business." Those words were true for us, in more ways than one. Our sales were increasing all around—in boots, Hats, and silver. Most important, we were improving our understanding of how to deliver terrific customer service. We were building a great reputation, allowing people to enjoy spending their money on quality goods, and to have fun while they were doing it.

Every week or so I would bring Bo, our Texas longhorn, into Aspen and actually ride him *into* the store. We would ride around Aspen and tie up outside one bar or another. For years we were a hit in the Fourth of July parade. We attended all kinds of parties and fundraisers for worthy causes, and we always encouraged people to get their photo taken with him. Since the Texas longhorn is so recognizable, people were quick to associate Bo with Kemo Sabe and the West.

Bo was once hired for an expensive corporate event at the Ritz Hotel in Aspen with the purpose of bringing him into the Grand Ballroom and letting every guest climb up on him to have their photo taken. To get to the ballroom we had to lead Bo through a maze of hallways and eventually through the kitchen, and then into the ballroom. Going through the five-foot-wide hallways and four-foot-wide doorways was a little complicated for Bo, since his horns were over six feet wide, so he had to turn his head sideways and make the best of it. He was a real gentleman through the hallways and in the kitchen, but things began to go to hell when he hit the waxed parquet dance floor and couldn't get any traction with his hooves—1,900 pounds of beef on ice skates! Nancy was able to get her arm around Bo's neck to calm him down, but she knew that he was desperate to ask her, "Why the hell is Yoder expecting me to do this, anyway?"

Then the CEO of the company showed up with a few drinks in him and decided that he should ride in on Bo and make a grand entrance. The problem was that he would have had a real hard time riding Bo in a pasture, even if he were sober. But I'm all for a grand entrance, so off we went into the cocktail party, with the CEO on Bo so that he could impress hundreds of his guests. For some reason, when he and Bo were directly under the gigantic chandelier, the CEO reached up and grabbed the bottom of it. He had his drink in one hand and was holding onto the chandelier with the other, and Bo just kept right on walking. So the guy, the CEO, slid off the back of Bo and was hanging from the chandelier with one arm while still holding his drink in the other hand. I reckon that he got what he wanted...a spectacular arrival to the party! Yee haw!

I can't remember who that CEO was, or what company he was with, but I wish I had kept track of him. I doubt that anyone has ever used words like timid or cautious to describe him. There is a Cowboy saying that goes:

"A true friend will come and bail you out of jail, but your best friend will be sittin' right there with you sayin', Wow, that sure was fun!"

My hunch is that he has been a "best friend" a few times in his life.

Nancy and I are so captivated with the Cowboy way of life, and the great American West, that we are always trying to use Kemo Sabe to show and tell about it.

During a trip to Wyoming, we became friends with a Cowboy named Bill Jones. Bill turned out to also be a Cowboy poet, and one of the most talented and fascinating people I have ever known. (You may remember that I reprinted one of his stories, "Snowmass Yuppie Talk," in an earlier chapter.) I was so intrigued by Bill that I convinced him to come to Kemo Sabe and hang out, simply because I liked him so much and knew that he would add to our Kemo Sabe romance. As Bill put it, "Well, I ain't never been hired to be atmosphere before, so I might as well do it."

Well, Bill became so popular with our customers, that we took the giant leap of trying to promote our own Kemo Sabe Roundups, with authentic Cowboy music, storytelling, and Cowboy poetry. Even though the few ticket-buyers who came to the shows thought that they were terrific, we just could never sell enough tickets to keep from losing a lot of money.

But we knew it was a great idea, so we kept at it. Stetson stepped in as the presenting sponsor, which allowed us to recruit Nancy's best friend, Linda Frosolone from Chicago, to be the director of the Roundups. Linda was absolutely fantastic with every single part of her job, right down to the minute details. Even though she was a city gal, she did her job by the "Cowboy Code," earning the trust of the best Cowboy entertainers in the West, and she was successful in bringing them to our shows. I still get chicken skin when I think about the heartfelt and sincere tribute that the Bar J Wranglers from Wilson, Wyoming, did for Linda when the curtain came down on the final performance. Every person who was involved in our Roundups, from the Cowboy entertainers to the stagehands, grew to admire, respect, and love Linda.

We held the shows in the legendary Wheeler Opera House in Aspen. We would actually load Bo into the service elevator, bring him up three stories, and have him on stage during the show! Bill Jones, with his dry humor, great stories and Cowboy poetry, was *always* the star of the show. But once again, the shows demanded so much attention, effort, and money, we just couldn't keep up.

Sure, we lost money doing our Kemo Sabe Roundups, but I'd do them again because:

- We learned so much about going all-out to do things "right." It was incredibly rewarding to do something so well.

- We became friends with so many terrific people.

- The shows helped us market Kemo Sabe as a store that believes in the Cowboy.

- It was *fun!*

After being on stage hundreds of times and telling his stories and Cowboy poetry in three books, Bill Jones pulled the plug on his entertaining career and went back to being a Cowboy. That's just the Cowboy way, I guess. But the Cowboy entertainment business just isn't quite as good without Bill.

Building A Team

"Motivation is simple.
You eliminate those that aren't motivated."
Lou Holtz

Finding and hiring good people is not only one of the most important jobs that you have in growing a small business, it is one of the most difficult. I can tell you from our own experience that you are bound to make some big mistakes when you hire people.

We sometimes hear a candidate tell us that we should hire him because he can "sell snow to a snowman." When we hear that, the chances of hiring that person are pretty much over. We don't want people who can *sell*—we are looking for people who want to be a part of our Kemo Sabe team and culture, and most important, are able to make the customer their priority.

Of course none of us want to make hiring mistakes, but even the best companies make mistakes, even at the highest level. On the bright side, hiring the wrong people can often lead to great stories about your business...

As I've already mentioned, every so often we take our team on a trip to Stetson, Lucchese, and Bohlin to see how Hats, boots, and silver pieces are made. On the last morning of the trip we always conduct individual interviews with the staff to determine what they learned and what they thought were the most significant elements of the trip. One guy, who was brand new, had given me the impression that he was way above learning about Hats, boots, and silver and barely interacted with any of us on the trip. He told me that the main thing he had learned was that the name Kemo Sabe was dead wrong for our store and that we needed to immediately rename the store "Baccarat" or "Cachet" because we carried such fine merchandise. He also gave me a list of things that Kemo Sabe was doing wrong, and said that he was the perfect person to turn things around for us. That rubbed me the wrong way, but we decided to at least give the guy a chance to work for us, in part because we had already invested quite a bit in him. It took only a few days before it was evident that he wasn't a team player and we cut him loose.

On that same trip we took another new hire, a woman who dressed, acted, and spoke as if she had lots of money and only wanted to work for Kemo Sabe because we were such a good store. Even though Kemo Sabe pays for practically everything on these trips, we realized that she hadn't brought any personal money with her at all. She was trying to walk out of convenience stores and Starbucks without paying, or she would snatch someone else's soft drink or bagel. After she worked in the store for a couple of days, we realized that she was "forgetting" to take off the expensive Hats, belts, and silver that she was "modeling for her personal customers" when she would leave the store. Obviously, she didn't last with us.

The lesson we learned was that you have to *earn* your invitation to go on one of our Texas trips, and that means being a Kemo Sabe employee for at least a year.

In both of our stores, Vail and Aspen, we love to have folks bring their dogs in, so we have a bucket full of dog biscuits strung up to the ceiling with a rope. It's a real simple operation to grab the rope, lower the bucket down to get the biscuits, then pull the bucket back up and hook the rope back on the wall. But in our Vail store, on the morning of July fourth, which is almost as busy as the week between Christmas and New Years, a young lady we had just hired eagerly lowered the biscuit bucket for a friend's dog. Problem was, after she pulled the bucket back up, she didn't attach the rope back to the hook on the wall and simply let go. Well, of course the bucket crashed down on her head. She spent the next week in the Vail Valley Hospital recuperating and getting all kinds of tests performed. In her opinion, this was entirely Kemo Sabe's fault. You can imagine how disruptive and expensive that was for us.

Now, I will tell you my absolute favorite Kemo Sabe employee story:

We were just opening our Vail store in June of 2004. We had the new Vail staff of five people come to work and stay in Aspen so that they would be ready to launch their store. One of the new hires was a lady who seemed to know more about *everything* than any of us who were trying to train her—you know the type—and it was apparent that we had made a mistake in hiring her in the first place. The lesson to be learned is that as soon as you realize and *know* that you have made a mistake, cut the ties and move on. This is always better for everyone. But we didn't. So on her second night in Aspen she decided to "borrow" a beautiful $750 30X silverbelly Stetson to wear around Aspen. The next day, she told us that she met a couple of guys at a bar who were too friendly with her and that she needed to toss her glass of red wine toward them. Well, not only did we hear from the owner of the bar, we also had a beautiful silverbelly Stetson that was ruined because it was soaked in Merlot.

And that's not the end of the story. We take a lot of pride in having high expectations of our staff and this, of course, requires detailed training. New members of our team generally tell us that the training is far more demanding, and more rewarding, than they expected. Well, this woman must have felt that the three days in Aspen were *really* stressful, because she threatened to file a lawsuit against Kemo Sabe for mental cruelty. As part of the suit she was going to ask for reimbursement for the twelve thousand dollars that she claimed to have spent on a Flight For Life helicopter to Denver because of the mental exhaustion that she suffered after training in Aspen. Well, of course that did scare me a little, because twelve thousand bucks is a lot of money, but when we talked privately with her attorney he confessed that neither he, nor any other attorney, would actually pursue her claims. I am not makin' this story up...how could I?

Sure, these mistakes make great stories, but when we consider the investment in time, money, and frustration that goes into making poor hiring decisions, the cost is astounding. It takes a lot of determination and endless persistence to build a team that will help you accomplish your vision of what you want your business to be.

It took many years, but we have learned to do a much better job of specifically defining a new position and exactly what we will expect from the new person. We now invite candidates back for second and third interviews. I remember that years ago I used to interview a person and project only the best scenarios about them. For example, I would somehow convince myself that the fact that they were late for the interview, or dressed poorly, was an exception rather than the rule for this person. I would say that they had done *something* right and that therefore I could teach them to be a great employee. Well, obviously that's a dangerous way of thinking when you're considering hiring someone. Now, we actually make a point of looking for flaws that could likely be a deal-breaker for the candidate's success at Kemo Sabe. That may sound harsh, but it is far better for everyone in the long run.

Wake Up And Smell The Coffee...Learn From Your Customers!

Your best inspiration for improving your store may very well come from what you think is an unlikely source—your customers!

We often hear other retailers or businesses say to us, "Well, Kemo Sabe is different *because* you are in Aspen and Vail." We sure don't buy into that because our customers are usually *not* from Aspen and Vail. They are from New York City to Dodge City; from Portland, Maine, to Portland, Oregon; from Palm Beach to Palm Springs; and from Boston to Austin, and every other town in the US of A. They are just like the customers that support so many other stores, restaurants, and businesses across the country.

Following are just a few of our favorite customers whom we have learned all kinds of stuff from...about business and service and determination. The problem is, to just name these few means that I am leaving out literally hundreds more who should also be on this list.

Leslie Wexner is one the most successful retailers in American history. Les has built Limited Brands into a ten-billion-dollar retail company that includes stores like Victoria's Secret, Express, Henri Bendel, Bath and Body Works, and The Limited. He is a loyal friend of Kemo Sabe and visits us often, and every time he does, it is an absolute thrill for me. What a compliment! It's like having Arnold Palmer call some average hacker to ask him how his golf game is.

Les has taught me so much, including the importance of paying attention to minute details. I will never forget when he said, "I like something about your store: I can tell who's in charge. Whenever I go unannounced into one of our stores and I can't tell who is in charge, I know we have a problem that needs to be fixed." Because of that advice from Les, one of our goals is to *always* have someone in charge, every minute that we are open. We call it the MOD, or "manager on duty." If that manager is not on the sales floor, we go so far as to have a MOM, or "manager of the moment."

Nancy and I recently went to a restaurant with one of the best reputations and best locations in Lionshead, Vail. Yet the service and atmosphere were absolutely awful. The reason was obvious to us: no one was in charge. Even though the restaurant and bar were busy, everything seemed to be out of sorts. The attention to detail was missing, including the appearance of the staff, who looked rumpled and sloppy. The employees didn't seem to have any interest in taking care of customers, or keeping the place clean or providing a great atmosphere. My hunch is that this wasn't all that unusual for this restaurant. Regardless of their location and how busy they sometimes are, this kind of careless attitude is bound to catch up with them.

Without Les Wexner's words of wisdom, I doubt that we would have been able to pinpoint the source of why this restaurant experience was so bad.

We got to know Mark Bezos as a customer before we realized that he was a partner in a small marketing and advertising firm in New York. We later hired the Bezos/Nathanson Marketing Group to help us with our advertising. They delivered, by far, the best marketing Kemo Sabe has ever done. Mark is one of those rare people who truly understands how and why Kemo Sabe operates the way we do. For our first project together, I invited Mark and his partner, David Nathanson, to meet our management team at the EA ranch near Dubois, Wyoming. We challenged each other to understand and define the core elements of success at Kemo Sabe. After spending three days in the saddle, then discussing marketing and customer service around the campfire in the evenings and over coffee at daybreak, we developed a helluva lot of camaraderie and respect for each other, which is still rewarding to this day. Even though Mark has moved on to the Robin Hood Foundation in New York City, I still ask him for his advice and opinions on anything that has to do with marketing.

Marc Cohen is an executive with the Taubman Company, which is one of the dominant retail landlords in the world. He works with the biggest and best national retailers, and even though Kemo Sabe doesn't have much in common with his classic retail clients, Marc has a sincere interest in us. We originally got to know Marc through his wife, Patti, who is one of our most loyal Kemo Sabe customers.

Marc is extremely talented with everything and anything relating to retail. He has an uncanny way of figuring out why some stores are so successful, while similar-type stores struggle. Every time Marc and I get together, our conversation turns to retail success, and I always come away with renewed inspiration and new ways to make Kemo Sabe better.

We actually had some pretty serious talks with Marc about Kemo Sabe opening a store in the Las Vegas City Center, which is managed by the Taubman Company, and will be one of the supreme shopping experiences in the world. I know that Marc stuck his neck out for us to be a part of their "point of difference" retail experience as a small specialty store among international retailers, but in the end we made the decision not to be in City Center. I often wonder how Kemo Sabe would have done on that stage.

Jerry Slusser grew up on a pig farm near Logansport, Indiana, not far from my hometown of Wabash. It is fascinating to hear him talk about driving the old farm pickup, with a hog or two, to the State Fairgrounds in Indianapolis. Back in the 1960s, Indianapolis wasn't a big city, but it sure did seem like a huge metropolis to Jerry. Jerry has more guts and determination than anyone I've ever met. Through hard work, perseverance, and self-confidence—which he attributes to growing up on a farm—and being dedicated to his favorite motto, *carpe diem*, Jerry has built an incredibly successful international business, especially with China. For years Jerry has been one of our best and favorite customers. It was only after talking with him numerous times that we realized we were fraternity brothers, only a year apart, at Purdue. I felt a little bad that I didn't recognize this, 'til Jerry reminded me that what you did yesterday isn't all that important compared to what you are doing today. *Carpe diem*!

I first met John Muse in our Snowmass store in 1992. He mentioned to me that he was interested in buying Stetson. Not *a* Stetson, mind you, but the whole company. My first reaction was, "Sure, this young guy is going buy Stetson? He's probably just a blowhard." Well, I couldn't have been more wrong. John Muse is definitely not a braggart or talker. He was raised in Texas and earned an appointment to the Air Force Academy. Actually, I'd say that graduates from each of the service academies have a lot in common with being a Cowboy because you need to be darn tough and you sure as heck can not BS your way through the program. John is an incredible businessman who loves Texas and the West, which is probably the primary reason that he owned Stetson for sixteen years and is still the principal owner of the Lucchese Boot Company. I have tried my best to learn how to exhibit John's most endearing talent: he has perfected the art and skill of executing authority in a gracious and respectful manner like no one else I have ever known.

Ramsay and Stevie Gillman are from Houston, where Ramsay is the owner of the well-known Gillman Automotive Group. In 1972 Ramsay had the vision, business acumen, and grit to sign on as one of the first Honda dealers in Texas. He went against the advice of almost everyone around him, who insisted that those Japanese imports were nothing but a fad and he would go broke if he tried to sell them, especially in Texas. Obviously, becoming a Honda dealer turned out to be a brilliant decision by Ramsay. In addition, Ramsay has been a leader in the automotive industry, serving a term as president of the National Automobile Dealers Association and ensuring that his Gillman dealerships throughout South Texas are committed to their communities.

Ramsay has had a home in Snowmass since 1982 and he and Stevie have been loyal to Kemo Sabe since our first year in business. Today, we should hire them on to provide atmosphere for Kemo Sabe.

Whenever they come in, the music volume goes up a notch, people are laughing, the place becomes even friendlier and *everyone*—our staff *and* our customers—is at their best. They just have that kind of effect on everyone wherever they go. If NBC had hired Ramsay, with Stevie as his sidekick, to succeed Johnny Carson as the host of *The Tonight Show*, he would have been a smashing success.

Bob and Varda Jablin probably rank as our most loyal and dedicated customers. They always wear some of their Kemo Sabe goods when they are in New York, Florida, Aspen, or wherever they may be.

Bob grew up in the garment business in New York and realized when he was young that he would most likely be following that career path. But because he was fascinated by the Cowboy lifestyle, he decided to attend Colorado State and try out for the rodeo team. Like, come on, Bob, get real, will you? Not only did he not know another person on campus, he was probably the only Jew in Fort Collins, Colorado, and was trying to compete in a situation where he had no experience! But because of his determination, persistence, and passion Bob made the team. It was with those same qualities and Cowboy spirit that Bob became wildly successful in the lace business, of all things.

Now, Bob and I saddle up together a few times a year for long rides through the backcountry of Colorado. I am fortunate to have such a determined friend; I believe that I become a better person every time that I am around Bob.

Cache Cache restaurant in Aspen is the epitome of fine dining. You feel genuinely welcome from the moment you walk in the door, and the atmosphere is as warm and inviting as can be found in any restaurant, anywhere. The ambiance is neither contrived nor manufactured, rather it is a result of the precision that Jodi Larner has used to build the success of Cache Cache.

Jodi is a customer and trusted friend of Kemo Sabe, just as Nancy and I are loyal supporters of Cache Cache. Jodi makes certain that there is a purpose and significance, down to the smallest detail, for every person and every article at Cache Cache. She has been the leader at Cache Cache since 1989, first as the manager and then as an owner. Through hard work and persistence she has learned to recognize everything that is taking place in her restaurant, and she knows how to take appropriate action immediately.

Cache Cache has an incredible staff. In a town where employee turnover is the norm, the Cache Cache team stays together, season after season. With Jodi's leadership they have mastered the art of delivering impeccable service without a hint of stuffiness or arrogance.

To me, above all else, the most important ingredient in the success of Cache Cache is the determination that Jodi has inspired in every person on the staff to make each guest feel important. I have never gone to Cache Cache and not been motivated to work a little harder to make Kemo Sabe better.

There is a similarity and common bond with every one of these people: each has a great deal of persistence, determination, character, and integrity. That's why I admire them so much and why I am so willing and eager to learn from them.

All of these people, plus many more I haven't mentioned, have played a huge part in making us a better store. As you know, at Kemo Sabe we look up to the Cowboy, and even though you may not find these guys on the back of a horse, they sure do qualify as Cowboys to us!

The Cowboy Code

The way a Cowboy does his job is a real inspiration to us. We figure that if Kemo Sabe uses the Cowboy as our role model, we will build a business that we are really proud of. At one point, our management team (James, Wendy, Gina, Nancy, and I) challenged ourselves to spell out exactly what we wanted and expected from each other and our staff. Nancy came to our next meeting with the following "Code of the West" that she got from Dave Stoecklein and James P. Owen in their book *Cowboy Ethics*:

1. LIVE EACH DAY WITH COURAGE
2. TAKE PRIDE IN YOUR WORK
3. ALWAYS FINISH WHAT YOU START
4. DO WHAT HAS TO BE DONE
5. BE TOUGH, BUT FAIR
6. WHEN YOU MAKE A PROMISE, KEEP IT
7. RIDE FOR THE BRAND
8. TALK LESS AND SAY MORE
9. REMEMBER THAT SOME THINGS AREN'T FOR SALE
10. KNOW WHERE TO DRAW THE LINE

I reckon that you could research every business book ever written and couldn't find better advice or wisdom than that.

I'm proud that Kemo Sabe has a connection to the Cowboy. And just think of how much better off the entire US of A would be if more of our business and political leaders concentrated more on living by the Code of the West rather than thinking of any possible self-serving way to get ahead.

The following stories illustrate why Nancy and I have so darn much admiration for the Cowboy, and the way that he does his job:

My good friend Darrell Winfield is a horse trader in Wyoming. Trading horses is a very tough way to make a living, and he doesn't run a big business. I initially went to find a horse from Darrell because he has built a seamless reputation for his knowledge, and even more so for his honesty.

A few years ago he made a large sale of horses to a wealthy guy with a ranch near Jackson Hole. The day the horses were to be delivered, the buyer's lawyer flew into Darrell's ranch in a helicopter, briefcase in hand, to get Darrell to sign some papers confirming that he would take back any horse if the buyer discovered any sort of problem. Darrell replied that the papers weren't necessary, since he guaranteed the buyer's satisfaction through his word, just as he has always done with every horse he has ever sold. The lawyer persisted, explaining to Darrell that without signing the paperwork, there was no deal. Well, Darrell stood fast, saying that his word was worth a helluva lot more than any papers could ever be. The end result was that after about an hour of the lawyer not understanding a Cowboy's ethics, and a Cowboy not comprehending that his word wasn't more valuable than a piece of paper, the deal fell through. How can you not admire a guy like Darrell?

By the way, Darrell Winfield is *the* Marlboro Man. Darrell has appeared in 80 percent of the Marlboro ads. Back in 1966, the famous Leo Burnett advertising agency came from Chicago to Pinedale, Wyoming, to shoot a Marlboro ad on the Quarter Circle 5 Ranch. Of course they brought their own Marlboro Man, who was actually a pretty good Cowboy himself, but when they needed him to ride down a brutally steep slope chasin' cows, he wasn't quite able to pull it off. Well, the ad *had* to be shot, so they asked a rugged young hand named Darrell Winfield, who worked for the Quarter Circle 5, if he would do it, and just like that, the legend was born.

The fact is, that era with Marlboro is one of the most successful ad campaigns in history. I'd say that the success is due, at least in part, to Darrell being a *real* Cowboy who did a whole lot more than portray a legend—he actually lived the life, and still does to this very day. That's the reason he was *perfect* for the role.

Darrell insisted, with a handshake agreement with Leo Burnett, that his first priority was being a Cowboy for the Quarter Circle 5, meaning that the Marlboro ads could not interfere with his job. He meant it, and stayed true to his word, even when he was the lead guy in the ads. He is a living legend and one of the best-known Cowboys in Wyoming—and not only because of Marlboro, but also because he has the persona, swagger, and manners of the American icon that he portrayed for all of those years.

Once when I was at Darrell's ranch he noticed that I was admiring one of his old saddles and asked me if I wanted to buy it. I told him that I did, but that I sure as hell didn't want to take another man's saddle. He said that he had too many saddles, and asked me to tell him what it was worth. That was an awfully tough question for me. See, I didn't want to offend Darrell and act like a snooty Aspen retailer by saying some high price (vintage saddles can be worth thousands and thousands of dollars), nor did I want to offend him by offering too little. After a few minutes, but what seemed like an hour to me, I blurted out, "Eight hundred fifty bucks." Darrell looked at me and said, "No, that's wrong...it's only worth five hundred." To this day, it is by far my favorite saddle and the one that I ride 98 percent of the time. I realize that its history, and the fact that it represents the Cowboy way of doing business, has a lot to do with why I like it so much. I also know that Darrell wasn't going to part with a saddle unless he knew that it was going to someone he respected. I'm proud of that.

Since he *was* the Marlboro brand, Darrell smoked nothing but Marlboros. In fact, he smoked 'em for fifty years, until the lawyers at Philip Morris decided that they might have some kind of liability. The very day that they informed him that he wouldn't be getting any more free smokes, he quit smoking. Just like that. Cold turkey.

Before Nancy moved out West she had a job in downtown Chicago. Every time she came up from the Illinois Central train station at Randolph Street and Michigan Avenue, the first thing she saw was a photo of Darrell on a giant Marlboro ad. Nancy says it caused her to dream about being out West, which always reminds me of the line:

"You never hear about a woman fantasizing about running off with an accountant."

Some other words of wisdom that I respect:

"If you have integrity, nothing else matters. If you don't have integrity, nothing else matters."

I always think of Darrell when I say those words.

The LX Ranch in the Texas Panhandle is one of the most legendary ranches in the history of the cattle industry.

Miles Childers, the owner, and Dave Anderson, who is just the *third* ranch manager in the past 105 years, are always gracious enough to let me come down and live the Cowboy life and at least *try* to be a part of a team of real Cowboys in action.

Dave has a saying: "It don't take long to spend the night at the LX," and I can assure you that it's true. I usually arrive at the Ranch well after midnight, and always find the same six-word note nailed to the bunkhouse door: "Be saddled and ready at 4:30." Period. Understand that when these guys work, they work. They set up camp out on the Ranch and congregate at the chuckwagon with a breakfast of eggs, bacon, flapjacks, biscuits and gravy, and coffee you eat with a fork.

The workday actually starts *before* breakfast, when the Cowboys catch and saddle their horses, which have spent the night in a large corral. Before even the slightest break of dawn, all the Cowboys form a circle around the horses in the corral, and without saying a word, one Cowboy at a time walks softly into the remuda, ropes his horse, and returns with his horse to the circle, until the last horse is caught. This method eliminates the chaos that would ensue if everyone tried to catch his mount on his own. Not only is this a darned effective way to get started for a hard day's work, it is a ritual that you would never, ever forget if you witnessed it with your own eyes.

What happens next describes why the American Cowboy is a living legend: It's just before daybreak, and even though there are fifteen or twenty Cowboys mounted on their horses, everything is quiet and still. The Boss, Dave, sits astride his horse in the center of the Cowboys, and in a barely audible voice, and with very few words, he gives the game plan to round up the herd and bring them in. We then trot off to gather a few hundred cows, calves, and bulls that have been grazing for the past few months in an area that covers thousands and thousands of acres. We ride for several miles through sage and mesquite, across gullies, drop offs and arroyos, through sand hills and juniper trees, all while we're trotting at a good pace. It's barely light, and the only noise is the magnificent sound of a remuda of horses as they are running together. Horse hooves, spurs, and creaking saddles. There is no whoopin' and hollerin' like in the movies. This is business, and there is simply no need to show off and act crazy. For a wannabe Cowboy like me, it's hard to describe how exciting and satisfying it is to be a part of this extraordinary experience.

After a few miles Dave waves off one Cowboy at a time until we have formed a long curved line of Cowboys and their horses, spaced a few hundred yards apart. Then we begin to slowly gather the herd. For the first hour or so, this seems amazingly easy, since there are only a few cows and calves. But soon, like a storm on the Texas plains, everything begins to change quickly and dramatically. There are now hundreds of cows and calves being driven through the gullies and mesquite thorns into the main herd. The dust and the noise of the bawling cattle is something that I reckon that you have to experience firsthand to comprehend. To add to the challenge, the bulls are fighting with each other, determined to keep their cows away from the competition. And there are always calves that break away to desperately look for their moms, who are somewhere in the chaos of the herd.

After a few hours the cows and calves have been herded into corrals and the *hard* work begins. First, the cows are separated from the calves, and since this is the first time that they've ever been apart, the bawlin' and cryin' creates a racket that words can't describe.

Next, a fire is built in the center of one end of a corral in order to get the branding irons red-hot. Now, two Cowboys, one on each side of the corral, mount up and rope one calf at a time and drag it back near the fire where young hands, called flankers, have the job of grabbing the calf, picking it up, throwing it down, getting it laid out, then holding it down for the stuff that's about to be done to it. Like what? Well, vaccinating, cutting horns, castrating, and branding. The flanker jobs go to the youngest Cowboys, usually kids who are still in high school. They always seem to be as thin as a stick and weigh about 110 pounds, but it is astounding just how tough and determined these kids are. The calves weigh anywhere from 125 pounds as a baby, to over 300 pounds for the ones that are a few months old. These kids who are doing the flanking get kicked in their shoulders and legs and sometimes in the head, but it's all part of the job, and they know it's probably not a good idea to let Cowboys like Jesse Ziegler or Chris Morton get kicked while they are vaccinating or cutting. It's a very long day for them, but they are learning to be Cowboys, and once in a while, towards the end of the day, the Boss will let them take their turn on their horse, ropin' calves.

The Boss (Dave) determines who rides and ropes, which is called dragging. Dragging is the best job, but also requires the most skill and partnership between a Cowboy and his horse. Tradition dictates that the first shift is awarded to the oldest hand, and next to a Cowboy from a neighboring outfit who might be there as a courtesy to the host ranch.

The Boss then assigns Cowboys to do the other stuff: flanking, vaccinating, notching the ears, clipping horns, castrating, and branding. Typical of the Cowboy way, there is hardly a word spoken by the Boss in appointing the jobs—little more than eye contact or a head nod.

It's downright amazing that to rope the calf, drag it to the flanker, vaccinate, notch the ear, clip off the horns, cut the bull calves, and brand, takes all of about thirty seconds. I'll flat tell you, these guys are good! The whole time, they are kidding each other about a mistake they made, or one of 'em gettin' kicked, or darn near gettin' knocked into the fire. It's *always* dusty, the wind is usually blowing, and it seems like it's either sticky hot or bitterly cold. In other words, it's about as far away as you can get from sitting in an office in the city.

It is astounding to me that even though Dave is always working hard in the middle of the action, he is also applying his knowledge and experience to manage a successful cattle ranch. If Dave's records show that they should have brought in 198 units (one "unit" is a cow and her calf) and he has counted only 195 units, he will work to find out where the missing three pairs are. Are they still out there? Did they somehow get through a fence? Or has something happened to them? He also takes a detailed look at every cow, calf, and bull to be sure they are healthy. Dave is an executive who is responsible for managing a vast and complicated business.

When the branding is done for the day and the cattle have been turned back onto the range, everyone makes their way to the chuckwagon where there are tubs full of ice, soda, Gatorade and a wagonload of beer. While the Cowboys are sittin' around tellin' stories, the cook will bring out plates piled high with calf fries, which are, of course, the nuts that were cut off that very day. It's pretty much the same as going to your local bar or restaurant for happy hour, other that we're sittin' on bedrolls rather than barstools, there isn't any primpin' going except for dunking your head in the horse tank to wash up, most city bars don't serve fresh calf fries, and instead of a sweet cocktail waitress we get the camp "hood."

Branding at the LX takes the better part of two weeks. Since the cook needs help at the chuckwagon with all kinds of chores like peeling potatoes and chopping wood, Dave will go into Amarillo to find a worthy volunteer to help the cook. He'll drive through the area where the homeless guys hang out and pick a fella willing to work for his board and a few bucks' pay. Over the years, he's come to be called the "hood," which is short for hoodlum. Sometimes he'll fit in, but it's not all that unusual for Dave and a few Cowboys to make several trips back to town to dump a hood off and bring another one back out to camp.

While the beer, whiskey, and BS is flowin', you may hear one of those Cowboys say, out loud, to no one in particular, "Can you believe we get paid for this?"

Get paid? Well, sort of…the Cowboy's day starts before 5:00 in the morning and ends when the work is done, usually around 6:00 in the evening. For this, the day-working hand (meaning that he doesn't work for one particular ranch but hires on wherever he's needed) gets paid around seventy-five bucks a day with no benefits whatsoever. In fact, instead of health insurance it's exactly the opposite: if you get hurt so bad that you can't work, well that's too bad. So if a Cowboy stubs his toe or something, he will tough it out and keep working. That's where the term "Cowboy up," which means to tough it out, comes from.

Here's just one story I remember from my time on the ranch: Since a Cowboy's knife is an essential tool for him to do his job, he will make darn sure that it's sharp—and I mean *really* sharp, like a razor blade. I vividly remember a scared calf jumping through the fire and crashing into Marty Crim, who is Dave's top hand. Somehow it caused Marty's knife to lop the tip of his finger right off. Even though it was bleeding like crazy, this apparently wasn't a big enough deal to get any special attention or slow down the branding operation. I did hear a few guys ask Marty what happened and his reply was something like, "Aw, nothin', I'm Okay." When I saw him the next morning and asked how his finger felt, he said, "Oh, like when you cut off the tip of your finger."

I can tell you for certain that being exposed to the Cowboy way at the LX, and being around guys like Dave Anderson, Marty Crim, Joe Brooks, Jesse Ziegler, Chris Morton, and Greg Stephenson has influenced the way that we run Kemo Sabe, and they have had a tremendous positive impact on our success. And that's a gross understatement.

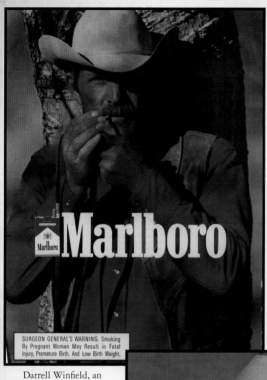

SURGEON GENERAL'S WARNING: Smoking By Pregnant Women May Result in Fetal Injury, Premature Birth, And Low Birth Weight.

Darrell Winfield, an
American Icon

Dave Anderson, LX Ranch Boss
Photo: Max Helmers

Yoder and Woodrow at
the LX Ranch in the
Texas Panhandle
Photo: Max Helmers

A young cowpoke takin' a break. This is our daughter Sara's son
Sam Milverstedt, with his pardner Roscoe.
Photo: Max Milverstedt

Wendy and Woodrow in a meadow at the LX Ranch

You can practically taste the dust and feel what it's like to move the herd at the LX.
This photo is one of my favorites.
Photo: Max Helmers

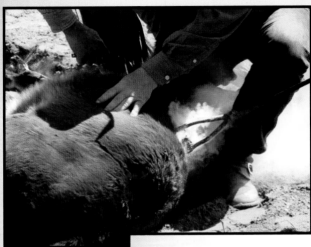

This shows that branding at the LX Ranch is no easy job

Branding at the LX. Marty Crim is on the left, Dave Anderson is in the vest

Dave Anderson double checking his tally book

A Cowboy's work is never done: our good friend Max Helmers
studying a trade journal
Photo: Jeff Vanuga

Nancy sent this postcard
to our customers in 1992
Card designed
by Frank Stransky

Early advertising. This newspaper ad was talked about for years

This ad from Mark Bezos and David Nathanson earned
some well-deserved national recognition
Photo: Jeff Vanuga

You don't get this
in the city
Photo: Max Helmers

Daybreak at the LX
Photo: Max Helmers

"If you don't know where
you're going, then any
road will get you there"
Photo: Max Helmers

Yoder and Roscoe near Aspen
Photo: Max Helmers

You've Got To Stand For Something...

It is incredibly important that small stores specialize in *something*. Let the giant retailers be everything to everybody.

One of the best retailers I've ever known is Tom Spiece, and I've learned more from him than I could ever begin to explain. Tom and I were high school buddies in Wabash, Indiana, and he went on to do extremely well with jeans and athletic shoes in his Spiece stores. Now he has made the move to online retail with a company he founded named Denim Express. He is the grand champion at thinking outside the box and he *always* relates to what the customer may be thinking. Tom, a.k.a. "the Jeansman," taught me that a small store needs to be *great* at something. And then, in addition to being great, you absolutely must prove it to your customer.

When the Jeansman walked into our little store in Snowmass soon after we started carrying Lucchese boots, Nancy and I were eager to see what he would say about our store, and especially about all of our new boots. We had displayed the boots in groups of two, three, or four pairs on little tables throughout the store. When Tom asked, "So, where are all the boots?" we couldn't believe what he was asking. "Well, they're here and there and all over the place...don't they look great?"

Later that day, after the Jeansman had literally taken our store apart and we began to put it back together again, I understood the lesson that he was teaching me: you had better darn well stand for something, and be great at it, or you're gonna get buried. In this case it was about showing our customers that we *believe* in boots. Since that day, Kemo Sabe has always featured an entire wall of boots, rather than a few here and a few there.

Another example is Cowboy Hats. We are nothing short of terrific when it comes to Hats. You should see our Hat training manual, or be a fly on the wall when we are training our staff. We know how Hats are made, how they should fit, and how to shape and trim them. Most important, every employee knows how to help the customer find the "right" Hat. And our training never stops.

I enjoy trying to figure out what percentage of people who end up buying their first Hat at Kemo Sabe have any intention whatsoever of buying one when they first walk in. I actually think the percentage is pretty low. Most of the time when a person buys something, they have at least some intent of buying that item before they visit a store. Yet, it sure seems to us like we are so good at Hats that what happens to our customers is something like this:

"The last thing that I'm gonna wear is a Cowboy Hat, so I sure don't need to go into that store.
Well, there's a lot going on in there, so I might as well go in.
Man, these guys are good.
Okay, I'll have some fun and try on a Hat.
Well, if I'm ever gonna buy a Hat this sure is the place.
Hey, I like this Hat and how I look in it and how it makes me feel.
I haven't felt this good about something I've bought for a long, long time.
Wow, I feel terrific. I love this Hat!"

Part of our training is based on the fact that most of our customers don't know much about Hats, including what they are made of, how to wear them, or even what size they wear. That's certainly not the case with boots, belts, buckles, and other goods that we sell. Everyone knows at least a little bit about boots and belts and buckles, including their size and what they are made of. So, we figure that if our sales team can become pros with Hats, then being successful with all of our other merchandise will be simple.

In addition to boots and Hats, Kemo Sabe is also exceptionally good with silver, belts, home furnishings, and accessories. We take a lot of pride in being at the top of the Western Retailer food chain with these products. At the same time, we are equally as proud of the fact that we DON'T carry clothing, which practically every other Western store in America is filled with.

Actually, a big chunk of our business used to include beautiful sweaters, leather jackets, vests, shearling coats, and stuff like that. Our clothing sales were pretty good, but we just weren't as passionate about this type of merchandise as we were about our Hats, boots, belts, and buckles. So we decided to give it up. We realized that we could be sacrificing 20 percent of our sales, but the darndest thing happened: our sales volume *increased* because suddenly we only carried goods that we strongly believed in! Today, when someone comes into Kemo Sabe looking for items that we don't have, we walk them to our neighbors, Pitkin County Dry Goods in Aspen, Axel's in Vail, or the world-famous Gorsuch stores, which are our neighbors in Aspen *and* Vail. Recommending our customers to other great stores allows us to concentrate on getting better with our own stuff.

The best example I've ever heard about trying to be "everything" occurred in London on New Year's Day in 1962. Four guys who were barely in their twenties had formed a rock band and were packing small-time bars in Liverpool and Hamburg. Eventually their manager was able to convince the mighty Decca label to give these kids an audition. But rather than playing their own brand of new rock, they chose to show off their versatility, including R&B, country, soft pop, cocktail-time ballads, and crusty old standards. The result was that Decca rejected signing the band to their label. By now you may have figured out that the band that Decca turned down was the Beatles.

Of course the Beatles were probably great at playing all kinds of music, and during that audition they tried to prove it by being *everything* for *everyone.* But in doing this, they failed to prove that they were *sensational* with the new type of rock music that they had created. Fortunately, they got another chance, and as you know, the rest is history.

I'm convinced that many small stores carry too wide of an assortment of goods, with the result being that they really aren't great at anything. When it comes to your business, always be certain that you are doing everything that you possibly can to be terrific at something. You can't be great at everything, so focus and direct your energy to being a star in one or two areas. Good things will happen when you are great at *something*.

Successful People Do Things That Average People Think Are A Waste Of Time

Because ski resorts are transient communities, coupled with the fact that I have never been known as an easy-going, happy-go-lucky manager, Kemo Sabe has had its share of employee turnover. Even though I have always known that a great staff is a critical success factor, we have sometimes had a difficult time keeping employees. It takes about a year for us to get a good person trained and indoctrinated into the Kemo Sabe way, but because we have so many young people on our staff, they often leave within two years. This creates a real problem. Keeping a terrific staff is actually our biggest challenge.

However, over the past few years we have gotten much, much better with the help of Gina Heinrich and Wendy Kunkle, two leaders who are fantastic at communicating with a young and transient staff.

Gina Heinrich. When you combine the following traits: listening *before* speaking, persistence, determination, creativity, remarkable communication skills, taste, vision, and extraordinary loyalty, you have the basic ingredients to clone a Gina. She represents a standard in the Cowboy Code: *Talk less and say more.*

Gina started doing odd jobs for Kemo Sabe, like wrapping packages and pushing a broom, when she was in eighth grade. She worked throughout high school and stayed in close touch with us every step of the way. Seventeen years later, she has taken on the responsibility of educating new employees on the way we do business at Kemo Sabe. Our training is one thing, but we also have very high standards regarding the type of behavior and attitude that we expect. Gina has an uncanny and highly effective way of getting the message across to our staff.

She also has zero tolerance for drama in the workplace. With every leadership position that Gina has held at Kemo Sabe she has been successful in eliminating the drama and sniping that is often harmful to a business.

Gina is also a champ on the sales floor. She is so good, in fact, that her business cards include the warning *"Watch Your Wallet"* below her name. Yet, one of the traits of a successful person, a professional athlete for example, is that he or she can easily cross over into a different sphere and be even better. Gina has done just that at Kemo Sabe.

If you are reading between the lines, or if you are one of our hundreds of loyal and faithful friends of Kemo Sabe, then I don't have to tell you that Gina is our daughter. (We also have another daughter, Sara, who lives in Oregon. Nancy always says that we have three kids: the two daughters, plus Kemo Sabe.) The truth is that Gina is sensitive about being the bosses' kid because she is so darned determined to make it on her own. But don't believe for a minute that Gina has it easy. We hold her to the same high standards as we do everyone else at Kemo Sabe.

Wendy Kunkle. I realized years ago that we needed a great leader on the sales floor to coach our staff on how we treat our customers. We hired Wendy in 2004, and the understatement is that we have that leader in Wendy. I could go on and on, but I wouldn't be able to convince you of just how good she is. For those of you who know her, enough said. If you're trying to hire a great leader, you may want to look for someone who has a background working in zoos, loves to race dirt bikes, and has actually climbed into the ring and boxed, 'cause those are a few of the things on her resume.

Wendy has a passion for knowing *everything* about our stores. She wants to know all about every customer and every bit of information about every piece of merchandise. A couple of years ago we were dreaming up ways that we could add a little more swagger to our Hats, and we hit on the idea of using the customer's initials to create a brand and burn it into the Hat. We ended up deciding that there were just too many problems involved to pull this off. But Wendy wouldn't give up; she was secretly working in her garage to figure out how to brand those initials into a Hat. Today, it is quite an experience to have us create your brand and watch as we burn it into your Hat, boots, picture frame, flask, or whatever you buy from us. Her persistence and determination with branding has added to the experience that we give our customers.

Wendy is proud to call herself the "Number One Bad Ass" and we kid her about being as soft as a fire hydrant, but I can assure you that beneath that tough skin is one of the most sincere, compassionate, and endearing people that I have ever known.

Because of Gina and Wendy, and with them working as a team, Kemo Sabe has become much better at selecting, training, and *keeping* great people. They have one trait in common: they are both absolutely loaded with persistence and determination. If you ever tell either of them that they can't do something, they are bound to work harder than ever just to prove you wrong. I feel confident about Kemo Sabe's future as long as we have Gina and Wendy riding with us. Of course, they fully understand that part of their responsibility is to recruit a few more stars that will be just as good as they are.

As far as my own leadership skills, I've given it a lot of thought, and I'm not sure where I stand. On the plus side, we have grown into a successful business with some fabulous employees, so if the end justifies the means, then I've done Okay. But I *know* that I have not been a great manager. I've been told that I set my goals, expectations and standards too high. Perhaps if I had been a little more tolerant, Kemo Sabe could have been more successful. I do know for certain that, as managers, Nancy and I have done one thing right: we have never been hesitant or intimidated about hiring fantastic people. Our goal has always been to train and encourage our staff to be better than we are. And it's worked—practically every person on our team can run circles around us in the way they perform.

I do have three specific expectations from each Kemo Sabe leader:

1. He or she must keep our stockroom neat and organized. I equate a retail store's stockroom to that of the mechanics and pit crew for an Indy Car team. A top-notch driver can have the flashiest car, but if his support crew isn't sending him out on the track with the best possible equipment, then he can forget about being competitive in the race.

    I learned that lesson years ago. Here's what happened to me: In the 1970s I was a young hot-shot buyer for the May Company Department Stores at May D & F in Denver. The president of May D & F, Jerome Nemiro, and Executive VP Dick Will, selected my coats and furs department to be one of the flagship areas to show off to May Company Chairman Stanley Goodman on his visit to Denver. Now you have to understand that, in perspective, Mr. Goodman's visit was like having the President of the United States come to visit some Mayor. I mean, talk about an opportunity for career advancement! For about a week my team and I worked like maniacs to make sure everything was perfect. But I made one hideous mistake: I used our stockroom as a dump and tossed everything from mark-down coats to cleaning supplies in there. The stockroom was such a mess that you could barely push the door open, let alone find anything you were looking for. So what does Mr. Goodman do when he arrives at my department? He walks briskly past me and my team and directly into the stockroom. I didn't get fired, but I knew I had let my bosses and my staff down. I was embarrassed and humiliated.

    However, I learned a lesson that I have never forgotten. That's why Kemo Sabe has wonderful, organized stockrooms with the purpose of supporting successful retail stores. I also know that I can tell you pretty accurately how successful a business is by the way the back room is kept.

2. I expect our managers to *think*. One of the most effective

things I do at Kemo Sabe is grab a cup of coffee and stand in the store by myself, before we open, and *think*. I try to see things the way a customer would, then I challenge myself to find ways to make us better. Try it. Pick out a small area, say ten square feet, or a countertop, and ask, "What is the purpose of this?" I guarantee you will be amazed at the improvements you can make.

3. I insist that our managers learn to write out their thoughts. This means writing summaries of their efforts to make Kemo Sabe better and what their goals and plans are for the future. Whenever we have an exceptionally great day, I need to know why—in writing. Through this, all of us realize that success goes way beyond luck. Of course, when we have bad days we certainly want to know what caused them as well. By writing, you *have* to *think*. There is just no way around it. If the most you expect from someone is a verbal recap or a quick explanation, then it's pretty darn easy to do it in a haphazard and cavalier manner...so why bother doing it at all?

I'm telling you about Gina, and Wendy because I am so darn proud of them. Each has contributed to make Kemo Sabe a better store than Nancy and I could have done. The moral to the story is that it is essential to hire honest, motivated, hardworking people, and after you have trained them, let them mature into stars.

Persistence And Determination

"Nothing in the world can take the place of persistence. Talent will not; nothing is more common than unsuccessful men with talent. Genius will not; unrewarded genius is almost a proverb. Education will not; the world is full of educated derelicts. Persistence and determination alone are omnipotent."

Calvin Coolidge

My favorite sports journalist is Peter King, who writes about the NFL for *Sports Illustrated*. I almost always find something in one of his articles that inspires me to make Kemo Sabe better. One of my favorites is his wrap-up of Super Bowl XLI when the Colts beat the Bears. He explained how Peyton Manning, the winning quarterback, stayed after every practice and threw hundreds of passes with waterlogged footballs so that he would be prepared on the off chance that it would rain during the game. Well, of course it rained, and of course, Peyton Manning had a great day passing, unlike the Bears' quarterback. Talk about preparation and determination...

You bet, persistence and determination are fundamental qualities for success in a small business. And beyond that, in my opinion, they are necessary qualities for a rewarding life. But, far better than me trying to preach to you, I can highly recommend three books, plus a movie, that are guaranteed to motivate you:

Kill Devil Hill, Harry Combs, 1979. This is the account of Wilbur and Orville Wright, and their determination to build and fly the first airplane. If you think that luck had anything to do with one of the greatest achievements in history, then you should read this book.

The Go Getter, Peter B. Kyne, 1921. This is a short story about a young man who was unwilling to give up. It was written nearly a hundred years ago, but it's timeless. Trust me on this one.

Endurance, Alfred Lansing, 1959. The incredible story of Ernest Shackleton's journey to Antarctica in 1914 and what it took for the crew to survive.

The Pursuit of Happyness (2006) with Will Smith.
This movie is a great example of Winston Churchill's quote: "Never give up. Never, never, never give up."

Swagger And Confidence

You haven't heard much about our Vail store, until now, because I have been all caught up in bragging about Kemo Sabe Aspen.

Imagine that someone opened a store right next to our Aspen location with similar boots, belts, buckles, and Hats. Well, I know for a fact that we would run that store out of town pretty darn quick. I promise you that we would give them a good, old-fashioned, butt kickin'. Why? Because having a *great* store goes above and beyond the merchandise and the location. In our case, it's about our *swagger*. We not only *think* we're good...hell, we *know* we're good!

We're good because we have a terrific staff. Every employee knows every piece of merchandise inside and out. Each one of us knows how to properly fit a pair of boots. We all know why a Hat is perfect for our customer or why it's not. And if it's not quite the "right" Hat, we know how to create one that is.

We are proud of every piece of merchandise that leaves our store. In fact, I can honestly tell you that when a customer buys something from us, we believe that we have just done something terrific *for him*, because we have just made his life a little better. This may sound backwards, but it's true.

Kemo Sabe Aspen has grown into fabulous shopping experience one day at a time, one customer at a time, and one employee at a time. But things don't always happen that way with a second location, in any business.

I may regret writing this, because it may bother some of our Vail customers and erode some of the confidence that they have in us. But the truth is that our Vail store was good, but it was not *great*.

"Good is the enemy of great."

That's the opening sentence of Jim Collins' fabulous book *Good To Great* (2005). I am very concerned that being "good" in Vail was holding us back from being "great."

We have a terrific location in Vail and have actually done a remarkable job thriving in what I used to call the Bermuda Triangle of Vail retail, because so many shops tried and failed in the same location. Sales are good. In fact, the time may come when Kemo Sabe Vail does more business than Aspen. But our Vail store just didn't have the same swagger and confidence of our Aspen store.

Was this the Vail team's fault? No, it was my fault, and *my* problem, because I had "wished and hoped" that Kemo Sabe Vail would develop the swagger and confidence that is the foundation of Kemo Sabe. But wishing and hoping just doesn't cut it. I had not made absolutely, positively sure that we gave our very best Kemo Sabe experience to every single Vail customer. We trained the Vail staff the same way that we trained our Aspen staff, but they did not have the "one customer at a time," day-after-day leadership on exactly how to deliver our special brand of Kemo Sabe service. This is an absolute necessity in building a *great* Kemo Sabe. The result was that, in Vail, our customers didn't get quite the legendary shopping experience that we give them in Aspen. But they do now!

I give you my word that Kemo Sabe Vail has become a great store, delivering a terrific shopping experience which I am proud to boast about. Our Vail store presentation, and even more important the staff and their service levels, make me proud to tell anyone and everyone to get into Kemo Sabe Vail and see for themselves.

Our Kemo Sabe Vail history actually dates back to 1998, when Nancy and I made quite a few scouting trips to Vail, looking for a potential location. We were confident that if we could find the right space, we could be successful in Vail. I remember getting calls from various real estate agents saying they had the "perfect" space for us, and that the opportunity wouldn't last long. We'd race over to Vail only to learn that, for one reason or another, we didn't consider it an opportunity at all. Then, in the summer of 2001, we saw a space that caught our eye. I vividly remember Nancy saying, "Yoder, if we move the front door, get rid of that stairway, and fix up the interior, this place could work for us!" Some of the other reasons we knew it would work:

1. It had a fabulous location right on Bridge Street, just past the covered bridge over Gore Creek that practically every guest uses to enter the Town of Vail.

2. It had a high ceiling that would allow us to generate our Kemo Sabe brand of atmosphere. See, we have become pretty good at showing off our hats by hanging them on ceiling beams and getting them down for customers by using a long stick. We also use the beams to hang stuff like old license plates, signs, and all kinds of other stuff.

3. Most importantly, it was owned by Rod Slifer. Rod Slifer is one of the reasons that Vail is on the very short list of "Best Ski Resort in the World." Rod has lived in Vail since 1963 and is an extremely successful businessman. He has served the Vail community in endless ways, including two terms as mayor, and is genuinely as nice of a guy as you will ever be fortunate enough to know. Nancy and I realize that the closest thing we have to a partner is our landlord, and even though we only knew *of* Rod Silfer, this "partnership" concept with Rod as our landlord made the space worth pursuing.

We had a hunch that the current tenant would be joining the list of failed businesses in that location, so we gave Rod a call, introduced ourselves and told him that someday we'd like to be considered for that space. Later, we learned that Rod had reached an agreement with Starbucks, which was a disappointment. We kept searching for a suitable Vail location, but without much success.

Then, in August of 2003 Rod called to report that, after months of negotiations, the Starbucks agreement had fallen through. The very next day James, Nancy, and I went to see Rod and within an hour we had a handshake deal, which was all that was ever necessary for either party.

Vail and Aspen are like the Red Sox and Yankees: they are both really good, but the understatement is that they have their differences. I assumed that when the various decision-makers and review boards in Vail realized that Kemo Sabe from Aspen was coming to town, they would roll out the red carpet, but I sure was wrong! I love an old Cowboy saying: "If it ain't broke you sure as hell don't want to be the one who finds out." To get what this means, think in terms of a horse. Well, the mutual admiration between Vail and Aspen wasn't broke, and I sure as hell found out. I spent some long hours in Vail's meeting rooms, answering what I thought were some absurd questions.

As an example, one of the review boards told me that the name Kemo Sabe was Okay with them, as was the print style of the logo. But the smoke signals, which are a part of our logo, wouldn't cut it in Vail. They said that Vail was a happy place, with clear skies, and that the clouds in the logo simply were not acceptable.

Then I was darn near run out of town when they discovered this message painted on our front door:

"If we're closed, just slide yer money under the door."

Things have calmed down over the years, but it took me realizing that I wouldn't be getting away with riding Longhorns and horses through the streets of Vail. In fact, my horses Frank, Woodrow, Roscoe, and I have been asked to disappear on several occasions. But, I am persistent and I'm pretty sure that we'll win them over any day now.

If You Wake Up And Find Yourself A Success, Then You Ain't Been Asleep...

Every small business is bound to make mistakes and suffer setbacks and disappointments. Learn from these mistakes. I know it sounds like an overused cliché. But I absolutely guarantee that when the wheel rolls around again and you get a "do over," you can be a smashing success.

For example, one of our signature Kemo Sabe items is our distressed Hats. These are new Cowboy Hats that we dirty up so that they look old and used, like they've been worn on the ranch. I'm proud to tell you that we are *great* at making these Hats. But it sure hasn't come easy. I distressed my first Stetson in 1992, and even though I was darn proud of it then, I can only imagine how bad it must have been in comparison to the beauties we make now. I would distress only one Hat at a time, because Nancy and I had no idea if they would sell or not. Then, when enough customers wanted a "used" Hat, the new challenge was *how* to distress them.

I started fooling around dirtying them up in the same way anyone would: I pulled all sorts of stuff out of the kitchen cupboards. Coffee, ketchup, gourmet mustard, barbecue sauce...I tried it all. I even used to carry a couple of empty buckets, a shovel, and a piece of screen with me when I was driving in Colorado, Wyoming, Utah, or

New Mexico and would often find places to prospect for the perfect dirt.

Well, even though I still get quite a few comments from people saying that they *know* how I do it, I can save you a lot of time, effort, and aggravation by telling you that those things didn't work for me and I doubt that they'll work for you either if you decide to get into the Hat distressing business.

Whenever I was on a ranch, or in a diner or honky-tonk—anytime I was around real working Cowboys—I would secretly study their Hats, trying to figure out why they looked so fabulous. Then, when I began spending a lot of time with Dave Anderson and his Cowboys on the LX Ranch, I began to understand how much Hats go through to give them their character. I'm not just talking about Hats either. I learned about boots, chaps, dusters, saddles—all of the classic, real Cowboy gear—that is vitally important to Kemo Sabe. Learning more about the stuff has had a fantastic impact on me.

After distressing a few hundred Hats over the next couple of years, I was actually getting fairly good at it. The problem was that I could only do silverbelly. Silverbelly is a silver-white shade that, along with black, is the classic Cowboy Hat color. I couldn't figure out how to distress darker colors like tan or chocolate, let alone black. No matter what I tried I just kept failing, time after time, when it came to distressing a black Hat. I would often believe that I had discovered the secret, only to learn that my new method didn't work and I would have to start all over again. I remember many times sitting up in bed at 3:00 a.m., waking up Nancy to tell her that I had a new idea, and then going out to my Hat laboratory, which was a shed in our backyard, only to realize that, once again, it wouldn't work. I ruined a pile of good Stetsons that were worth a lot of money. I donated most of them to the local thrift shop, and once in a while I will actually see someone wearing one.

Finally, years later, I stumbled onto the secret sauce. Now, more than half of the Hats that we sell are distressed, and they are pretty well evenly divided between silverbelly, black, and brown. So, all of my experimentation has been worth the frustration that I went through. I still make every distressed Hat myself and I'm very proud of that.

Our Risky Way Of Bonding With Our Customers

At Kemo Sabe we take a lot of pride in running the place the Cowboy way. It's one more way of staying true to our word to make the customer feel important. For example, we are always pleased to help you out. That could mean fixin' up your Hat, getting some much-needed conditioner on your thirsty boots, polishing your silver buckle set, or just giving you directions to wherever you're wanting to go. You can always get a great cup of coffee or a cold beverage, and we're sure as heck not expecting you to buy anything…it's just our way of saying welcome and howdy.

But sometimes a customer comes in who feels the need to prove that he is extremely successful back home. These customers are almost always from one big city or another. Even though we are friendly and try to talk with them, we are often quickly and abruptly told that they don't want our help because they already own lots of boots or Hats or whatever. Well, we take this as a challenge and try to soften them up and encourage them to enjoy themselves. Often, this involves some teasing, but our staff has gotten so good at it that we almost always accomplish our goal of getting people to actually have fun while spending money!

Nancy is generally the most gracious person on our team. Yet on occasion, even she can come very close to pushing our style of service a little too far. One busy afternoon, with every salesperson balancing several customers at the same time, a guy walked in and sort of elbowed his way up to Nancy and said, "Hey, can't someone give me a hand?" Without saying a word or missing a beat, Nancy gently put down the expensive silver buckle set that she was showing to customers and began to clap, slowly and deliberately. It took about seven seconds before everyone in the store was giving this poor guy a hand. At first he was madder than hell. Steam was coming out of his ears and you could have fried an egg on the back of his neck, but within a minute or two he was laughing and joined the Kemo Sabe "inner circle" with everyone else. Obviously, this kind of "service" is very dangerous, but our successful employees have a way of pulling it off and making it part of our Kemo Sabe brand.

We also like to kid people about their Black American Express cards. With a Black AmEx, which has no credit limit, you can buy pretty much anything you want, no matter how expensive, right on the spot. A few years ago there were only a handful of Black cards in circulation, so when someone would whip one out we would ask, "Who are you, anyway?" Then we would ring our cowbell, which we do when we have some sort of announcement (like, should this person buy this Hat? Yes or no?) and report that there was a Black card in the store. Only once did a customer mind this treatment, but that was only temporary, because the guy kept coming back time after time, using his Black card for even very small purchases, and expecting to hear the cowbell every time!

It is amazing how often we see people loosen up and enjoy themselves at Kemo Sabe in a short amount of time. We are on a never-ending mission to convince people to trust us, and it's rewarding when we see that we have succeeded. Sometimes, rather than us actually selling anything, there is a party going on right in our store, and as long as you're friendly, then by all means, you're invited to join in.

One thing we don't like is people hammering us for a deal. That can put us in a foul mood because we like the premise that *everyone* pays the same fair price. We just don't give deals, regardless of whether you are a "friend" or are spending a lot of money or are one of our best long-time customers. We decided years ago that giving deals was a very slippery slope that we just didn't want to be on.

And that includes "locals' discounts." This charade has gotten way out of hand in resort communities. How insulting do you think it is to someone who is paying full price to realize that other people are getting a discount? And where do you draw the line as to who is a "local"?

I'd like to tell you that I have been polite to every Kemo Sabe customer, but that's just not the case. A few years ago I overheard a guy, who was with his wife and another couple, tell the rest of the foursome that he could get them the local's discount by saying that they were from Aspen. He said that since they "looked like locals" we would never know the difference. Since I take so much pride in our honesty this put a burr under my saddle. After a while, they wanted to buy two inexpensive straw Hats, but *only* if we would give them a deal. That definitely wasn't gonna happen, but they kept badgering us 'til it *should* have been downright embarrassing for them, especially since there were quite a few other customers watching. So I rang our cowbell, and announced that we had some people who wanted these $35 Hats but just couldn't afford them, and asked everyone if they could contribute some of their spare change to help them out. Well, as you can imagine, the two couples left in a big hurry, madder than hell at me. The next day, however, they came into the Vail store and when they learned that Nancy was the owner they told her about the jerk working in the Aspen store. Without admitting that I was her husband, she assured them that she would fire me immediately. They were so pleased that they bought the two Hats without asking for a deal!

Minding Your Store

Competition is great for your store. A little competition keeps you motivated and on your toes. Besides that, it's really fun. Many stores put a lot of effort into "comparative" shopping, analyzing their competitors' merchandise and prices. At Kemo Sabe we don't invest any time or effort into worrying about what other retailers are doing. We know that we have more than enough on our plate running our own store, so why should we worry about the other guy?

Similarly, a lot of stores spend an enormous amount of time and energy trying to arrange exclusives with vendors. They meet privately with the supplier and say, "If we buy your product will you promise to not sell to anyone else in town?" Or even better, "You can sell your line to other stores around here, but only the stuff that we decide *not* to buy." Boy, I can't tell you how appealing it is to have a salesman tell you that you can buy his line, but only the goods that some other store didn't think were good enough for them.

Kemo Sabe won't have anything to do with letting some other store dictate what we buy. We have also had a policy since day one not to ask for brand exclusives. We want to do business with suppliers who have enough confidence and expertise to select their vendors and determine the best way to have their product represented by retailers. I'm not so sure about the value of exclusives anyway, especially now that anyone can shop any store in the country from their own computer.

We dedicate a lot of time and effort to our relationships with our vendors. However, our conversations aren't always warm and fuzzy, and there are times when we need to push our suppliers to perform up to our standards. For example, we get extremely irritated when our orders are not shipped on time. We are very specific as to when we want our goods to arrive and it drives us nuts when we hear excuses from our vendors telling us that they got swamped with other orders, didn't have the materials, or got too busy because of the holidays. This really frustrates us because it means we're unable to take great care of *our* customers.

As with any business, we are constantly struggling with the *quality* of our goods. Sometimes the shade of the color will vary enough to turn a winner into a dud, or the fit isn't exactly right, or the workmanship isn't up to the standards that we expected. And the response from our suppliers that really irritates us, but one that we hear way too often? "No one else is complaining..." On one hand, it gives us a sense of pride, because it means that maybe other stores just don't care about their products or their customers as much as we do. On the other hand, it sends a warning that the supplier may not be as committed to their product as we are, and that we may not be able to depend on them.

My advice to businesses that encounter problems with vendors is this: stand up for your store and for your customers, don't accept inferior quality, and don't settle for anything less than committed service from your suppliers.

And here's a little note to suppliers: if you have a store that desperately wants to carry your line, you should think real hard about giving them a chance. The odds are that their determination will outweigh the reasons that you have for denying that store to carry your line.

Back in 1992 we were passionate about representing the Lucchese brand in our Snowmass store. I called and wrote countless times, asking them to give us a chance. I promised that if they ever came into Kemo Sabe, they would be truly honored to have us represent them. Of all of the times I tried, I never even got the courtesy of a response from a Lucchese representative—not even, "No, go away and leave us alone." My good friend in Indiana, Tom Spiece, who was a Lucchese dealer, stuck his neck out and put in a Lucchese order for us, then sent the boots to Kemo Sabe. This is called diverting, and is really a nasty way to do business, but I *knew* what a terrific job we could do with Lucchese and I was desperate.

With that, they finally acknowledged us, and of course we got in a lot of hot water at first. But now, I am proud to say that we are one of Lucchese's premier stores, not just in sales but also in the way we represent the Lucchese brand.

Ride 'Em Like You Stole 'Em

An acknowledgement to a few people who have been so important to Kemo Sabe. We couldn't have done it without them.

One of the most rewarding parts of my experience at Kemo Sabe is the opportunity to get to know some incredibly talented and fabulous people. My favorite business friends are those who combine business success and expertise with their personal Cowboy ethic. The Marlboro Man Darrell Winfield and Dave Anderson from the LX Ranch are certainly on that list, plus a few others that I need to tell you about.

Neil Sutherland. True, Kemo Sabe has grown into being one of Lucchese's premiere retailers, but we didn't build our Lucchese success alone, or even with Tom Spiece. We were fortunate enough to be dealt a great hand: we had the best sales rep in the entire Western retail industry, Neil Sutherland.

Unfortunately, Neil is not our rep anymore, but he was absolutely terrific at three things:

1. Loyalty
2. Attention to Detail
3. Service

For example, Neil would analyze Kemo Sabe's boot sales and find that we sold more black boots in smaller sizes with narrow toe styles, while brown boots were the opposite. He made many, many trips from Arizona to teach us about boots, and even more important, about how to build a strong and loyal relationship with our customers. Neil is one of the best people I've ever known and he has had an important influence on Kemo Sabe. Without Neil we wouldn't be nearly the boot store that we are now!

Chet Vogt. For thirty-five years Chet Vogt has built a very successful business with Vogt Western and Silver, his sterling and leather goods company. But it's even more of a compliment to Chet that he is also an exceptional cattle rancher. His absolutely fantastic ranch near Elk Creek, California, is not only beautiful, it's also widely acclaimed for Chet's dedication to the environmental stewardship of the land. Through my time spent with Chet over the years, I have not only gained invaluable education about horses and the land, we have also become fast friends.

Sad, but true: They just don't make 'em like Dick Maday anymore. Dick's passion is Stetson Hats. He cares more about Stetson than any person I have ever known. Dick has hundreds of pieces of Stetson memorabilia from classic Hats close to a hundred years old to original posters and crazy stuff like lunch pails and ash trays. Heck, Dick actually loans his collectables to the Stetson Hat Company.

You've Heard the saying "Do what you love and love what you do!". Well, this is the description of Dick Maday because he has been THE BEST Stetson sales rep for some 40 years and has played a huge role in our Hat success at Kemo Sabe. The Stetson "salesman of the Year" is aptly named the Dick Maday Award!

Dave Marold. The name Bohlin is legendary in the Western culture. Edward Bohlin set the standards for anything and everything associated with Cowboys and silver when he started Bohlin Silver in

1920. Now, the brand is entrusted to Dave Marold of Dallas, who is as dedicated and determined as any person I have ever met. Our staff also has great respect and admiration for him. Here's what Wendy said about him:

> *"Of course, I love Dave Marold. He always gets us what we need and expedites everything! He makes our customers and me feel important. He also helps me with the staff. I swear, after he helped Clay with his presentation, Clay became a different person! I really trust Dave. I also like that he is always looking outside of the box—much like Kemo Sabe."*

Although he's the owner, Dave is also directly involved in the smallest detail of every piece that Bohlin makes and is committed to having Bohlin do its very best for every customer. Dave lives and breathes the brand. Dave Marold *is* Bohlin Silver!

Clint Orms. Clint is acknowledged as being one of the finest Western silversmiths alive today. Being with Clint is like being transported back in time a hundred years. Yet, like Kemo Sabe, Clint Orms Silversmiths is anything but a one-man show. Clint's wife, Roxie, runs the business side of the operation and is one of the finest CEOs I have ever worked with.

There are a few other individuals who play a major role in Kemo Sabe's success and whom we are proud to call our friends:

- Margy Davis of Lucchese.

- Brittain Roberts, who supplies us with Hatbands and accessories through her own company, Indigo Cowgirl.

- Dan Fitzgerald, the owner of Wild West Braiding.

- Heather Dillard of Moore & Giles Leather Bags and Accessories.

- Debbi Sherman and Joni Duncan of Vogt Silversmiths.

- John Holden, the Hatman, who is also the president of the National Bit, Spur and Saddle Collectors Association.

- Ken, Patsy and Duane Miller who own and operate one of the best customer oriented businesses that I have ever encountered, The Horn Shop in Fort Worth, Texas.

- Jeannie Meckstroth, who was our original store manager in Vail and is still a vital part of the Vail team. Jeannie is as loyal as any person I have ever known, and there is no finer quality than loyalty.

- My three friends, trusted confidants, and business advisors: Scott Blackmun, David Mize, and Richard Tegtmeier.

We have also had many terrific employees, but the reality is that some of the truly outstanding ones have been kids who have just finished school and are not interested in a retail career, so they move on after a year or so. Kemo Sabe has practically been their family in a town that is a minefield for young kids, so when they leave it is a tough parting for James, Gina, Wendy, Nancy, and me. We have also learned so much from their youthful confidence and exuberance. The good side of it is that we know we have had a positive influence on them and that they are on their way to succeed in whatever they want to do. I would like to name every person that has added to Kemo Sabe's success and reputation, but that would be an impossible task.

Yet, three people do stand out as my favorites and I'm pretty sure that every one of our customers who ever met any of them would agree: Colleen Tuohy, Kaycee Orr, and Fast Eddie.

Colleen Tuohy. Colleen had this laugh and personality that helped make Kemo Sabe a great store. Whenever she was in the store we had a whole lot more atmosphere and fun, not to mention increased sales volume. When the bigwigs of the worldwide edition of United Airlines' in-flight magazine, *Hemispheres*, met "Cools" in the store, she made such an impression on them that they used a full-page close-up photo of her in the magazine, with her bright eyes and terrific smile lookin' straight at you from under her Stetson. Heck, no wonder the Ralph Lauren/Polo people recruited her to move to

New York and work for Polo at the Mansion, where she is now a floor manager.

Kaycee Orr. In addition to having the best attitude of anyone who has ever worked for us, Kaycee brought Kemo Sabe a wealth of knowledge about Hats. She actually grew up on a ranch, in the Hat business, working for her Aunt Susie, who owned the Greeley Hat Works, founded in Greeley, Colorado, in 1909. She has a personality that, when combined with her authentic Cowgirl great looks, just flat out causes you to like her immediately. Add those attributes to her loyalty, work ethic, and character, and you can see why Kaycee is one of my all-time favorites! Unfortunately for us, she got swept off her feet by Jason Hoffman, a rancher from California, and they are now running their own cattle ranch in Thedford, Nebraska. Kaycee now owns her own Hat company called Bar None.

Fast Eddie. When someone is far and away at the top of their profession, say an athlete like Michael Jordan, you will hear people say that he is a "natural." Of course, to get to the very top and stay there takes an incredible amount of hard work and determination, but still, a lot of natural talent has to be there to begin with. When it comes to Hats, I have never encountered *anyone* who has the talent of Fast Eddie. He has the taste, the eye, the personality, and the swagger to make anyone look his absolute best in a Hat. To him, getting someone in a Hat is an art. When Eddie tells you how great you look, you believe him!

Fast Eddie's real name is Ed Golub. He came to Aspen in the early 1970s and later started a little Hat shop he called, of course, Fast Eddie's. As good as Kemo Sabe is with Hats, Fast is still Aspen's Hat Man, and he always will be. After Eddie closed his shop in 1999 he joined our team and had a huge positive influence on everyone at Kemo Sabe. We still get an amazing number of people telling us that they bought their first Hat from him. I nominated Ed for the Aspen Hall of Fame and to this day I am still irritated that he has not been inducted. He shaped the destiny of a town that is known all over the world for its shopping—he was the most popular retailer in town.

David Stoecklein Says It Best

David Stoecklein is probably the most accomplished Western photographer of our time. He claims that he is not really a Cowboy, but I disagree. He *lives* the life and you will often find him in the saddle. David is 100 percent Cowboy, inside and out.

Simply looking at his photos is a wonderful experience, but when you *study* his work you can't help but be captured by the romance and passion of the Cowboy and the American West. He is one of the most talented and determined guys that I've ever met.

Fortunately, "Steck" has published nearly fifty books, filled with narratives, stories, and his photography. I encourage you to acquire a couple of his books and make them a part of your home—I guarantee you will be glad you did.

Here is an example about just how small this great big American West is: In passing, Steck mentioned to Nancy that he was working on a new book about the greatness of the American workforce, and that he had already decided who was going to be on the cover. Well, it was none other than Dave Anderson from the LX Ranch, who Steck said was the toughest Cowboy he has ever known. And this was *before* Steck knew that we even had any idea who Dave Anderson is, let alone that he is one of our very best friends!

The more experience I gain, the easier it is for me to admit it when someone can do something better than I can. So, rather than me telling you how important the Cowboy should be to American business, I am including this description of the Cowboy, written by David Stoecklein as the foreword of James P. Owen's *Cowboy Ethics.*

People often ask me what it is about cowboys that makes them so different from the rest of us. They want to know why the West and cowboys stand out as symbols of American culture and values. In my mind, it is because cowboys live by the Code of the West, a code of honor and truthfulness. They live in a world where a man's word is his bond and a handshake is enough to seal any agreement.

The West is a place where the fence is always tight but the gate is always open to friends and neighbors. It is a place where a man can make tough decisions without looking over his shoulder or worrying what someone else will think. A cowboy gets his strength from knowing what is right and what is wrong and being true to his beliefs. This is the essence of the Code of the West and the true cowboy way.

Cowboying is not just a job, but a way of life.

I am proud to say that we have made the Cowboy Way a part of Kemo Sabe. We have always tried to treat our customers, suppliers, and staff with respect, and no one has ever needed anything more than a handshake to do business with us.

As I mentioned earlier, this book is not some complicated or detailed formula for building a successful small business. But, by doing our best to figure out how to keep our customers happy, Nancy and I have created our own brand of success, and you can too.

My simple advice is this: try applying the concept of *MTCFI* to your own business and running your business the Cowboy Way. You will be amazed at just how rewarding it can be.

Thanks to everyone—it's been one terrific ride.

Tom Yoder